Ferdinand C. (Ferdinand Cartwright) Ewer

Catholicity in Its Relationship to Protestantism and Romanism

Being Six Conferences Delivered at Newark, N.J., at the Request Of...

Ferdinand C. (Ferdinand Cartwright) Ewer

Catholicity in Its Relationship to Protestantism and Romanism
Being Six Conferences Delivered at Newark, N.J., at the Request Of...

ISBN/EAN: 9783337007782

Printed in Europe, USA, Canada, Australia, Japan

Cover: Foto ©Lupo / pixelio.de

More available books at **www.hansebooks.com**

Catholicity

IN ITS RELATIONSHIP TO

Protestantism and Romanism

BEING

SIX CONFERENCES

Delivered at Newark, N. J., at the Request of Leading Laymen of that City

---

BY

THE REV. F. C. EWER, S.T.D.

Milwaukee:
The Young Churchman Co.

TO THE

REV. S. BARING GOULD,

WHOSE TEACHINGS IN THE CHURCH HAVE LENT COURAGE
AND INSPIRATION TO THE AUTHOR,

THIS VOLUME

IS

GRATEFULLY DEDICATED,

BY HIS BROTHER IN THE CATHOLIC FAITH,

F. C. EWER.

TO THE READER.

THE Addresses in this volume were prepared and delivered in compliance with the following request, signed by some thirty laymen from every Parish in the city of Newark, N. J., viz.:

"Impressed with a conviction that the Word of God sets forth a distinct System of Truth, which is held and fully taught by the Church; and also that a clear understanding and reception of the Fundamental Teachings of the Christian Religion are necessary for the proper development of man's spiritual life; and, further, convinced that a desire exists on the part of many earnest-minded men to know of a System of Faith resting on a surer basis than individual opinion, we, laymen of the Church in Newark, respectfully invite you to deliver in our city a series of Conferences on the Church as the Custodian and Teacher of Divine Truth, in opposition to ultra-Protestantism, and to the anti-Catholic claims of the Papal Church."

To this request the following reply was sent, viz.:

NEW YORK, April 24th, 1878.

GENTLEMEN :

I was yesterday in receipt of your communication, requesting me to deliver in Newark a series of Addresses on Catholicity in Its Relationship to Protestantism on the one hand, and to Romanism on the other.

I understand from the gentleman who brought me your communication, that your desire is to have the Conferences delivered on the Wednesday evenings in May and early June; and that three of them be on the subject of Catholicity in Its Relationship to Protestantism, and three on Catholicity in Its Relationship to Romanism.

I do not fail to recognize the importance of this call; first, in the subject it suggests, and secondly, in the number and high standing in the Church and in the community of the citizens by whom it is signed. And I desire to thank you for the confidence which it extends to me.

Your call comes at a time when I am very much pressed with Parochial duties; and in justice both to the subject and to yourselves, I could have wished to have the comparative leisure of the months of June, July, and August, in which to prepare the Conferences you desire.

But on the assurance of the gentleman who bore me your letter, that you would be entirely satisfied, and would not deem me discourteous, should I use material for the first three Conferences which has already been used and is somewhat known to portions of the public, I comply with your request; and will endeavor to be with you for the first address on Wednesday evening, May the first.

With great respect,
Your obedient servant,
F. C. EWER.

However, on further consideration, the author resolved not to use any of the material contained in his volume on "The Failure of Protestantism," as that work had already passed through several editions, and would, moreover, have furnished to his hand sermons, rather than such religious addresses calculated for a secular audience, as the request called for.

In preparing the following addresses from week to week, therefore, as they were delivered, he has endeavored, by the development of an argument which begins in the First Address and does not close until the end of the Sixth, to show the sceptic, first, why he should be a Christian rather than an Infidel, or a Unitarian in belief; secondly, a Catholic rather than a Protestant; and lastly, an Anglican Catholic rather than a Roman Catholic.

In compliance with the request of a number of

those who desire to have these Addresses in book-form, a Sermon has been added, which the author was invited to prepare and preach last year before the members of an Evangelical Parish, in explanation of the Object and Meaning of the Catholic Movement in the Anglican Communion.

CONTENTS.

FIRST CONFERENCE.
    Catholicity, a Continent of Certainty; Protestantism, an Ocean of Conjecture........................... 1

SECOND CONFERENCE:
    Catholicity, a Life and an Organizer; Protestantism, a Disorganizer and a Death.... 43

THIRD CONFERENCE:
    The Catholic Church, both Perfect and Imperfect.—Leaves Room for Play of Mental Activity.—Catholicity, the "Yea" of Christianity; Protestantism, the "Nay."—True Cause of Protestant "Reformation."—Protestantism, Diversity without Organic Unity; Rome Organic Unity without Diversity; Catholicity, Organic Unity in Diversity........... 74

FOURTH CONFERENCE:
    Functions of Reason in Religion.—Recapitulation.—Catholicity in History.—Which is the Catholic Church?—Difference between the Catholic and the Roman Idea of the Unity of the Church. The Roman Idea essentially the same as the Protestant.—The Roman Idea not sustained either by Scripture or by History............. 129

Contents.

FIFTH CONFERENCE:

Constitution of The Catholic Church in Its Priestly, Sacrificial, Prophetic, and Regal Functions.—Romanism overthrows this Constitution.—The Church's Government Episcopal, not Papal.—Gallicanism a Logical Mistake.—Hierarchy within the Catholic Episcopate. — Papal Supremacy not Sustained by Scripture 166

SIXTH CONFERENCE:

The Papal Autocracy not Sustained by History.—Caution with regard to Papal Controversial Books.—The Theory of the Anglican Church, Catholic, though Her Present Ritual Practice be Uncatholic; The Theory of the Roman Church, Uncatholic, though Her Present Ritual Practice be Catholic.—Prophecy touching Rome's need for Conversion, and Her Three-fold Denial of Christ.—Conclusion..... 219

SERMON:

The Object and Meaning of the Catholic Movement in the Anglican Communion........ 267

NOTES.

N. B.—This edition has been carefully corrected from notes made by Dr. Ewer on the margins of his library copy; but the following additions could not be conveniently introduced into the body of the book.

Page 41, line 7, after "Himself," add "But how do we know that this is the Body of God on earth? Gentlemen, there is and has been no other organic form in time that claims to be God's earthly Body. If then it must be that He is on earth in a body somewhere, this alone must be that Body. If He is on earth, surely that Body in which He is visible would be self-conscious of its pre-eminence among all other earthly organisms. But no other than one only, viz., the Catholic Church, claims this pre-eminence."

Page 171, line 2, after "Ordination," add "takes a member of the Church and binds him into unity with His Priestly body."

Notes.

Page 172, line 11, after "Body on earth," add "Christ's Real Presence in Heaven and Christ's Sacramental Presence on our altars."

Page 226, line 15, after "it is all novel," add "Thus when a Protestant rouses up to run headlong away from Protestantism, Rome by the simplicity of its system readily catches his attention, his comprehension and his acceptance."

Page 263, line 4, after "He knew that," add "those who would be called."

CATHOLICITY, PROTESTANTISM AND ROMANISM.

FIRST CONFERENCE.

CATHOLICITY, A CONTINENT OF CERTAINTY: PROTESTANTISM, AN OCEAN OF CONJECTURE.

GENTLEMEN,

The most solemn question a man can put to himself is, What is Truth? We are somewhere in a universe of complicated fact and intricate phenomena; but where? We exist now; but where along the flow of the eternal is that "now" set? In this universe, whose bounds we know not, complexity pervades every part; it is within us, it stretches away behind the farthest stars, it comes up to us from an eternity behind, and goes on to an eternity before us. All the facts and phenomena of this vast and intricate scene move with perfect harmony, because guided by the great single will of God. All, do I say? All but man and demons. Set in this universe, to act in discord with its laws and complex movement, is misery, disaster and death. To move in accordance with the All is peace, success, life. Now, to have the order of ideas within correspond with the order of fact and phenomena without, is to have within us the Truth; this, therefore, is to have the means of life. To have the order of ideas within not correspond with the order of phenomena without—this is error; and acting on it is disaster, misery, death.

You have not come up here to consider the correspondence between the order of ideas within and the order of all fact and phenomena without. Scientific, political, financial, artistic fact and phenomena you care not for; for this world passeth away. No, the correspondence you wish, is that between the order of ideas within and the order of those unseen facts and phenomena that lie beyond the limits of the natural and below the horizon of time. What is Truth there? Your question is a question, then, of life or death. We have to live but once; we have to die but once. How shall we live aright?. How shall we die aright? Once only can we shape our course for eternity. It is according to error or according to truth. It is either to sail into correspondence everlasting with the complex facts and phenomena of the eternal and the supernatura., or to sail into a miserable discord with them; it is either, then, unto life, or unto that whose only fitting name is death. For, an extraneous particle, caught in a vast machine and out of harmony with its movements, is but crushed and ground by the resistless, ceaseless action of that in which it is set. God, time, eternity, and all that fills them—this is the vast machine in which you are set. You have come up here, therefore, to ask, What is Truth? to seek to bring the order of your ideas into correspondence with the order of supernatural fact and movement, external to yourselves, unalterable and eternal.

But a question is "an hunger." For who would ask for what he already has? Three hundred years ago Luther and Calvin announced that they had the Truth. But the stormy seas of private judgment and of human criticism upon which they launched it, and the detective solvents of inexorable logic which they challenged, have been too much for it. Calvin cannot answer Channing; Channing cannot answer Parker; Parker cannot answer Frothingham. Lapsing time, too, hath brought its strain upon it; lapsing time, which is the Divine criticism on all systems, hath confronted it with unexpected situations, hath stretched it upon new problems for which, in its human infirmity, it had not foreprovided ; and, lo! it is rent and gone to pieces. After three hundred years you behold it a miserable raft, its fragments floating apart like the mere flying rack of the heavens. And you behold poor remnants only of the great nations clinging to its parted and broken logs, and earnest thinking men at their wits' end to know what is Truth. It is a question of the preservation of Christianity on earth.

Let me pause here a moment. How is it that I am summoned here by citizens of widely variant views? What has happened in the last ten years ? The world does not stop. Truth may be drowned by the cries of ridicule ; but the hearts of the silent people, who are watching it, are ever loyal to it, even in its degradation on Calvary ; and there is no device yet discovered that shall transubstantiate, in their eyes, either ridicule or prejudice into argument. In 1868 the solemn Indictment against Protestantism, drawn up in the fear of God and in behalf of dying souls, and uttered from Christ Church, Murray Hill, was met, not by argument, but only by a gale of holy malediction and impotent scorn. But those who felt with the penman of that Indictment have bided their time. For there is no device yet discovered that can prolong the life of an excitement, and save it from sinking into a calm in which the quiet voice of argument can again be heard. I look around, and, lo, ten years have wrought a change. In St. Louis, in Wisconsin, East and West, the challenge to Protestantism is taken up again and begins to swell. And here, in 1878, I call you to mark the pregnant fact, that, as that Indictment was not in a single instance answered in 1868, so it has not been answered since. And here, as a priest of God Almighty's Catholic Church, I call again from these steps of His holy Altar for an answer to that Indictment, if it can be given.

If any one claims again that steamboats and cotton mills are Protestantism, one can only say that again the claim calls for no notice. Protestantism a failure? Why, look at your lucifer matches, your locomotives and suspension bridges! And one, gazing with sad eye upon the five points of Calvinism, upon the Lutheran dogma of justification by faith, upon the rule of private Scriptural interpretation, upon absolute predestination, effectual grace, final perseverance and infant damnation, looked away from Protestantism as he was bidden, and observed the patent reapers and sewing machines, and failed to see the connection. No one ever charged the inventive faculty of man with being a failure when acting in the natural realm. It was the inventive faculty of fallible man operating in the supernatural realm, and substituting there a human for a Divine contrivance of salvation that had failed.

In short, the attempt was made to identify Protestantism with the Nineteenth Century ; and, because the Nineteenth Century was clearly a success, to non-suit the indictment against Protestantism. This was shrewd, but not sagacious. With many it succeeded for a time. Grave critics in newspaper and magazine flew at the volume of sermons entitled "The Failure of Protestantism," condemned it out and out, declaring in the same breath that they had not even read it, and did not need to. One eminent New York clergyman received a service of silver plate from his parishioners, for proving that the Nineteenth Century was not a failure, and that Romanism was an error; neither pastor nor people having the slightest conception of the comical attitude in which they had placed themselves.

No one had charged that the Nineteenth Century was a failure, or claimed that Romanism was true. Protestantism is something that exists in modern times ; now, if not only modern times, but also everything that is in modern times, are successes, then are the Comtean school of Positivism, and Emersonian Pantheism, and Spiritualism, and Fourierism and Mormonism successes.

Protestantism was set up as the Cause of all the glories of the Nineteenth Century. What! the religious dogma that says : " Away with God's Apostolic visible Church, and let every man be his own church, his own Priest, his own interpreter of the Bible, and his own judge as to what the Bible is," the cause of all this science and modern light?

The real cause of the light and advance of modern times is not a theological dogma which had its birth in the Sixteenth Century. But it is the human mind, which began to awaken into activity far back in the middle ages, four hundred years before the Protestant dogma was thought of. As that human mind began to arouse out of its sleep in the Eighth Century, it began to be prolific. It abandoned the rude structures of those ages, and brought out, long before the Continental Reformation, the most ornate specimens of architecture the world ever saw; in the Eleventh Century it invented paper, and produced printing before Calvin and Luther saw the light ; in the Twelfth Century it devised banks of exchange and discount, and, not long after, invented gunpowder, conceived the idea of the post-office, discovered and applied the principle of magnetism in the mariner's compass, and thus gave such a start to commerce and geographical discovery as they had never had before; it invented painting in oil-colors before Luther was born; in the Thirteenth Century it introduced astronomy and geometry into Europe, and, not long after, brought in algebra also, and fostered all three sciences; it produced a Dante, a Petrarch, a Chaucer, a Boccaccio and a Roger Bacon, long before Luther was born; five hundred years before Calvin and Luther, it established free schools for the country urchin and the town child; centuries before, too, it gathered up out of the Gothic and Vandal ruins the precious literary treasures of Greece and Rome; and founded universities at Oxford, Cambridge, Bologna, Vienna, Heidelberg, Paris, and innumerable other cities.

No, the cause of the light and advance of modern times was this general awakening and ever increasing activity of mind; an activity which began far back in the tenth century or earlier; which not only brought out all this that I have mentioned, but more also; which has been bringing out new blessings to man ever since; which has rolled up and out a thousand things

—most of them good, some of them bad; which, after a while, rolled up the Protestant dogma as one of its many and varied inventions; and which is rolling up to-day in England and America the solemn presentment of that dogma and of its disastrous fruits at the bar of this enlightened century.

Now there are those who would have one think that Protestantism is not merely one of the heterogeneous mixture of things, which, awakening mind in its power, but also in its fallibility, turned up, six hundred years after that mind had begun to produce its marvellous fruits, but that it really is, somehow or other, the cause of all the good of modern times, gunpowder, glass, paper, printing, painting, telescopes, astronomy, algebra, Magna Charta, and everything else. This were to suppose a mother producing children before she was born. Protestantism was but one of the effects of the general awakening of mind, not its cause; and our charge is that it happened to be one of the bad effects—not in that it struck at Roman error, but because it has destroyed Catholic truth also. "Where Protestantism prevails, there everything prevails which blesses mankind; *ergo*, Protestantism is true." This is the argument. Nay, it should have been said that where active mind prevails, there thousands of things prevail which bless mankind, and some things that are curses. Where Protestantism prevails, quotha? Why, one might as well say where Spiritualism prevails, where infidelity prevails, there everything prevails that blesses mankind: ergo, infidelity is true

To say nothing of the specifications in those eight Murray Hill discourses, what were two of the main counts in the Indictment? First, that whereas, two hundred and fifty years ago, the Protestant religious dogmas held captive to themselves great thoughtful peoples of the Germanic, the Swiss and the Anglo-Saxon man, those dogmas had failed to retain the hold they once had, and have, to an overwhelming extent, lost, at last, the intellect of those peoples: and that, while two hundred and fifty years ago Protestantism held the masses as well as the intellect of those peoples, it has failed to hold and has lost those masses as well as the intellect: that Protestantism, as a form of Christianity, stands to-day breast-deep in torrents of skepticism, which itself hath let loose, which are deepening around it, and in which it is drowning; and that it stands there to-day aghast and incompetent. This was one count in the Indictment. Gentlemen, you have seen that it has not been denied.

A second count was that the fundamental religious

premises of Protestantism were essentially anti-Christian, and must end, by inexorable logic, in infidel conclusions; that if Calvin's and Luther's and Zwingli's premises were to be accepted, then Channing's conclusions were nearer right by logic than Cromwell's, and Theodore Parker's nearer right than Channing's, and Frothingham's and Adler's the rightest of all, and quite unanswerable by a Protestant: that when the Calvinists burned Servetus at the stake, they burned Calvin's own brain-child. It was furthermore claimed that if this logical aspect of Protestantism was correct, it ought to have shown itself finally in practical historical results. And the charge was made that what thus ought to have followed logically, had actually followed historically, and was patent to all in the comparatively empty churches and the widespread skepticism of thoughtful Germany, America and Switzerland. This was another count.

I reiterate: with all that was said ten years ago on the subject, in sermon, newspaper and magazine, not then did any one, not at any time since has any one come candidly up and grappled with these two main counts in the Indictment. Can they be met and answered? If so, why have several editions of the volume containing the Indictment been allowed to be read, openly or secretly, (for the volume was forthwith placed on the Index Expurgatorius of Protestantism) and to work like leaven in the community for ten years? If they cannot be answered, it is not strange that earnest-minded citizens should arise and ask, What is Truth?

To resume; those who say to the world, "We have the eternal truth," speak, of course, with authority; and that authority must be one of two things, either baseless or founded on a rock. Protestantism cried, "We have the Truth," and nations listened. What strange thing do you at once behold as the nations clustered to the chair of Protestantism? I will tell you. The tones of Protestantism to the world were the tones of authority. It summoned the people to itself to instruct them. And yet it asserts its own fallibility. Every religion which does not at least claim for itself infallibility, convicts itself by that fact that it is liable to lead men astray in that solemn concern which, fixed but once, knows no cure. Behold, then, this amazing event—the dying nations flying for the eternal truth to a system that proclaims its liability to plunge them into error. For such a system to teach in the name of a God, Whose truth is one, fixed and eternal, and Whose ways alter not, nor conflict with each other, is the consummation of the absurd. No, gentlemen, as Jesus Christ was the only human being who dared to call himself God, so Catholicity is the only Christian body that dares to call itself infallible; that dares to begin its discourses, to give its truth, to pronounce its judgments and to pardon sin, "In the name of the Father, and of the Son and of the Holy Ghost." The Sovereign Lord God hath Himself prepared a remedy for Protestantism; and that remedy is the anarchy with which it rends its own domain in a sublime suicide. And so it lies writhing under the human, and dying under the Divine criticism.

Out of the sixteenth century, then, there sounded the cry, "We have the Truth." We have listened to that cry and have seen what has come of it. It was a cry of mere human voices.

On the 18th of July, 1870, that cry sounded again to the world. It arose, not from the plains of Saxony, not from the lakes of Switzerland, but from beneath the shadow of the Apennines. This time it was in the singular number: "I alone have the Truth." All mankind are bid to note that an august Prelate, when speaking from his throne as doctor, and instructing the world in faith or morals, is infallible. But, nevertheless, gentlemen, you have heard that second cry, and have turned your ear away from the Vatican. And do I do other than speak your thoughts aloud when I give the reason why?

If we are to yield our own ideas and accept, without arguing, what is told us as the truth, we must first of all be convinced that we have reached the fountain from which only eternal truth flows. In short, reason is truly called by Catholicity "the prelude of faith." Why, then, is it that, since the 18th of July, 1870, we are all to believe that the Pope is infallible? Prior to that date the world did not believe it; voices which spoke from high places in even the Roman Catholic hierarchy itself "had declared that this doctrine of Papal Infallibility was not and could not become an article of Catholic faith. Not only had the once powerful school of Gallican divines emphatically repudiated it; not only had Roman Catholic bishops and clergy in Ireland, not very many years back, put on formal record their denial of it; not only had such an approved manual as Keenan's Controversial Catechism declared it to be no article of Catholic belief, and affirmed that no Papal decision could bind, under pain of heresy, unless received and prescribed by the teaching body of the Church; but many European bishops had, in recent times, distinctly denied it to be a part of Catholic doctrine; and American bishops, just before the Council and during the Council, had expressed their conviction that it was out of harmony with both Scripture and tradition, and that it contradicted the history of the Church as a teaching power."

And yet on and after the 18th day of July, 1870, we are told that the 170,000,000 of Roman Catholics accepted the Papal Infallibility. Something must, then, have happened on that 18th day of July eight years ago as a reason why the world is called on to believe the Pope to be infallible. What happened? A solemn dogmatic decree was promulgated. That was all. Who promulgated it? It was the Pope himself, the Patriarchal Council approving. Ah, then, the decree rests upon two supports, the Pope and the Council. Let us examine each support. And first the Council. The Council, as one of the supports of the decree, was either fallible or infallible. If it was fallible, then, for all we know, it may have made a mistake when it announced the Papal infallibility. But if, on the other hand, it was infallible, then, by asserting something else and not itself to be infallible, it has infallibly pronounced its own fallibility. Indeed, the decree itself declares the Council to be fallible :

for it says: "The definitions of the Roman Pontiff are, of themselves, *and not in virtue of the consent of the Church*, irreformable." If, then, the Council, by its own admission and by the Pope's assertion, is liable to error, we have no guarantee whatever that it spoke the truth when it taught that the Pope was infallible. Thus, either way, one of the two supports on which the decree rests—namely, the Patriarchal Council—proves utterly rotten and worthless.

Reason is the prelude of faith. Let us pass, then to the other support on which the decree rests—namely, the assertion of the Pope himself. Prior to the 18th day of July, 1870, the question to be decided was whether or not the Pope was infallible. On the 18th day of July the Pope himself settles the doubtful question. How? Why, by simply declaring that he is infallible. Is this logic? "I am infallible." Why? "Because I am infallible." Behold here, gentlemen, born in the womb of an occasion most illustrious, and issuing from a gathering which, for stateliness, robed splendor and solemnity, has rarely had its equal, this flagrant instance of the fallacy known as "Begging the very question at issue;" an instance which is perhaps the sublimest in its presumption and the most absurd in its simplicity that the world ever stood amazed at

There are people in this world thoughtless and discourteous enough to say that the feminine mind has some peculiar notions of its own touching logic; that if you ask why a certain thing is so, a reason, entirely satisfactory at any rate to itself, is "Because." One is reminded, *mutatis mutandis*, of what the able critic of *The Church Times* said of Cardinal Manning. One "does not know whether such ungallant suggestion be well founded or not in the case of woman; probably not. But it applies with singular force" to the promulgator of the above decree.

What connection there may be between the angry portents of heaven and the deeds of man in the moral and intellectual realms, who shall say? That the former are rolled out of the physical realm coincidently with the occurrence of the latter in the moral realm by that God, Who holdeth and guideth both realms as one by His one will and power, may be too much for science to fathom, but not too much for faith to receive. At any rate we know what God hath said : "And there shall be signs in the sun and in the moon and in the stars ; . . . for the powers of heaven shall be shaken." At any rate you have seen Melchior, Gasper and Balthasar guided to the spot where the young Child lay. And, at any rate, we know that darkness came at noon-day, while the Jews were accomplishing their purpose. When on the 18th day of July, 1870, the aged man, crowned with the tiara, arose with great form and pomp from his throne in the Vatican Basilica, and made the awful declaration to the universe, "I alone have the Truth," above the dome of that Basilica without, there had already gathered out of the reservoirs of the air a storm, which those who saw it describe as almost unequaled in blackness and turmoil and terror. And as the poor, feeble human voice lifted itself from earth, it spoke into the deepest gloom, and was instantly answered from heaven by angry flashes of the most blinding lightning and peal on peal of sudden thunder, as though in a Divine derision to drown the Pontiff's awful words.

From the University of Wittenberg and from the lake-shores of Geneva and Zurich we heard the cry, "We have the Truth." But it was only the cry of human voices, claiming no infallibility. Again from the banks of the Tiber it arose, "I have the Truth." But it was again the sound of a poor human voice only; a voice claiming indeed infallibility, but the claim based on supports both of which crumble to dust at the touch. And so you have turned your ear away from the Vatican.

But a question is not only "an hunger," it is also "a hope." For who would ask for what he despairs of ever having? And so you have come up here with the great question on your lips. Have you seriously asked yourselves why you have come up here? Is it —since you cannot rely upon having the truth from Rome, from Geneva, from Wittenberg—in order to sit at the feet of another mere man, and be instructed in new dogmas of grace, justification and salvation, which he, too, has excogitated and deems correct? No, gentlemen, you have not placed me in so absurd an attitude. You announce that you have already had enough of the mere fallible human voice crying to you, "Put your trust in me."

There is a second explanation, then, of your presence here; and does this account for it? Having, namely, in your minds the various statements touching grace, justification, the atonement and salvation, which men have propounded as the Truth, do you come here for still another theory, in articled, dogmatic statement, in order that you may sit as judges, weighing the new with the old, and decide which is the most Biblical and probable, or select parts from all and form another theory to suit yourselves and perhaps to announce to the world? But this would be merely using me for new material, and then falling back on yourselves for the Truth; while there is that within you which, in its hunger, cries, I have not the Truth to give, nor power to summon it forth, nor reagents to test it. No, gentlemen, in coming up here, as you have not placed me in a mortifying position, neither have you placed yourselves in so absurd an attitude.

There is only one more explanation. You will neither trust me nor yourselves. Ah, then, gentlemen, you seek no less than the Divine voice to give you the Truth. But do you expect to hear the Divine voice speaking the Truth to you through me to-night? No. For we accept the Divine voice without arguing; and you have come here to consider, to weigh, to reason. To consider what? Reason is the prelude of faith; and you have come up here to reason within yourselves and to consider whether there be anywhere on earth any channel of the Divine voice, any audible source of infallible Truth, and if so, where you are to find it. For such and such only will neither deceive nor fail you; with such and such only will you be satisfied; before the presence of such and such only will you be at rest. Then, having accepted, without arguing, the Truth from a source that will not deceive us, we may afterward reverently examine and admire its pearls and rubies, and compare them with the diamonds of glass and the emeralds of paste.

If there be on earth the audible Divine voice, where shall we go to find and listen to it? This is the question of to-night. It is very difficult to disengage one's self from the influences of education and from long habits of thought. Ideas and prejudices which we have gained in our childhood, youth and early manhood from our parents, from the Bible, from the atmosphere of Christianity around us, root themselves into us until they become almost a part of the very fabric of our minds. And yet I am going to ask you to join with me in the difficult task of utterly disengaging yourselves for a brief while from all impressions of every name and nature touching even God, which you have had all your lives, and touching the future life, revelation, Christ or salvation. They may all return upon you when I have gotten through; but for the nonce let us put them all away in order that we may come with virgin minds to a certain pathway where I wish to take you. In that one pathway at least we wish no disturbing elements, no shadowy forms of previous notions and prejudices beckoning us hither and yon, as we cautiously move on. Then we shall be all alike as we enter. It is a pathway of very simple reasoning; and I beg each one of you to examine carefully every single link in the chain from first to last.

Why is it necessary for me to ask you away from all your previous impressions into this pathway at all? It is because we are, with our different educations and religious influences, all in confusion; and I desire that we go back and start even, and all over again, without a Bible, without a Christ, without a Church, without Sacraments, without any religious notions— and see where we shall come out.

Let me say, in the first place, then, that as we stand surrounded by the innumerable sects and forms of Christianity, the plain man is utterly bewildered with the conflicting voices. He thinks there are a thousand and one questions which he must carefully and painfully settle if he would get out of the maze and reach the truth. No, gentlemen, this is a mistake. Numerous as the forms of Christianity are, and certainly their name is legion, they fall as inevitably and infallibly apart into classes, orders, genera and species, as do the innumerable flowers of the vegetable kingdom. Settle three questions and your trouble is gone. The first two are not difficult or complex questions either. And it is up to them that I would bring you face to face to-night.

Now all chains of reasoning must hang upon staples. It is impossible to conceive of a chain of reasoning extending back infinitely into the past and hanging nowhere. In the mathematics, reasoning starts from axioms. I start then with certain statements which I ask you to admit without proof. I ask you to admit: (1) That there is a God; (2) That that God is a perfect God of love; (3) That we each of us exist; and (4) That our senses give us tolerably accurate intelligence of that by which we are surrounded. Bear in mind, gentlemen, that we all admit that God is a perfect God of love; for that is of importance. Indeed, Voltaire himself once said, that even if there were no God, it would be necessary to invent one. If you do not admit this, then I have nothing further to say. If you do admit it, then I go on; and let us see where we shall come out. I do not ask any of you to take a single step where you cannot follow; but having taken any step, I simply ask you, in this course of Conferences, not to go back.

We all start even, and therefore I will take some one of us, not as a guide, but as a specimen for each of the rest; and let that one be myself.

I exist, then. And, looking round about me, I find myself in a vast temple. Above me is its mighty dome; spread out beneath me is its vast floor. It is the Temple of Nature. How did I get here? (Remember, we have wiped out all our previous religious impressions.) How did I get here? I know not. I only know that I entered it through the gateway of birth, and that I shall go out of it through the gateway of death. Within this Temple of Nature I find innumerable objects, and I find physical, mental and moral laws operating. I can observe and group its facts, form theories, test my theories by experiment, ascertain its laws, and come to fixed and certain conclusions, in which I can rest and on which I can act. For I have senses which place me in connection with all around me, and enable me to be intelligent concerning the abode within which I am enclosed. I know that I shall exist here but a few years, and then I shall go out of this temple through the doorway of death. Whither shall I go? I cannot see beyond, and I do not know. I can follow a fellowman up to death; but the moment he has passed away my faintest whisper, my loudest cry does not reach him. He is gone from me as completely as though he had been suddenly annihilated. I stand and rap at the door of death; what is there beyond? I listen; there is no reply. Is there an existence beyond and outside of this Temple of Nature? If so, will my existence be eternal or not? Are there rocks and dangers there for me to escape? What are the beings that live in the realm of super-nature? Moreover are there invisible facts and phenomena and laws that prevail *here* in the supernatural? I know not. How then am I to know the Truth with regard to the latter that I may so shape my course here as to enter upon a successful existence there? I know not. I am completely cut off from them by the walls of nature. I cannot see them through those walls; I cannot hear their sound and movement. If I form theories about them, I cannot bring those theories to the test of experiment; and so I am totally cut off from ascertaining whether my theories are true or not. How then am I to act here with certainty? Standing at the door of death, I can, indeed, conjecture concerning those facts, phenomena, laws and requirements in which I may be living now and into which I am to plunge; I can conjecture about all the unseen supernatural that plays here in this Temple of Nature; about the law of the forgiveness of sins and justification, and the means of salvation. And so, too, can another man conjecture. And his mere guess, though it contradict mine in every particular, is as good as mine;

for both our guesses are mere guesses, and are really worth, so far as certainty is concerned, just nothing at all. Why sow seed in cloud-land? Why waste time! Let me turn back, then, from the door of the supernatural here and hereafter at which I am standing to this Temple of Nature, where there is something positive; where, if I form a natural theory, I can test it by natural fact and come to some settled and positive conclusion. As for supernatural fact and law and process, we, shut up as we are in this Temple of Nature, are all by nature drowning in an ocean of mere fruitless conjecture and guesswork.

And yet, if I am to live eternally in the realms of the supernatural and among its phenomena and laws, if its laws play here unknown to and unseen by me, and have a bearing upon me, then, that I should have no guesswork, that I should be able to bring the order of my ideas within into harmony with the order of those supernatural facts, phenomena and laws, that I should have no less than the positive and infallible truth concerning them, this, to me, is of the vastest importance. It were the most exquisite cruelty to shut me in here and leave me drowning in an ocean of mere conjecture about eternity and its laws and requirements. My danger of unending disaster is enormous; for truth is one, like the centre of a circle, while the possibility of variation from it and of error, is infinite like the radii that point in every direction. This, then, is my situation by nature.

Now, just here, gentlemen, I call you to take the first step along the pathway with me. It is this : God is love; I have admitted that. Therefore there is no escape from the logical conclusion that He *cannot* leave me in my miserable plight of fruitless guesswork. He cannot leave me in my awful position of drowning in an ocean of mere conjecture and incertitude about topics, concerning which it is of the vastest importance that I should have knowledge no less than exactly true; for anything short of infallibility itself in the matter leaves me still in uncertainty and danger. I can run no risk whatever where the stake is so fearful, because eternal. God is love; and the first conclusion is, He must and has done something to help me. And, furthermore, it must be that in helping me He will do so effectually, *i. e.*, He will make no mistake. He is not going to attempt to help me, and cheat me by leaving me worse off than before. For He is perfect and knows what the real help will be, and all-powerful and able therefore to effect it, or He is not

God at all. Being God, then, and infinite Love, He must, can and has helped me, it may not be to all truth, but to such truth at any rate as is essential to my case, and has somehow helped me effectually to this truth.

Is there any flaw in this first link? I cannot see any; and I seem to hear you say, "No; go on."

Very well—the next point is *how* has He helped me? Gentlemen, there are only three ways possible and only three ways thinkable. One is so to place me that I can help myself in this matter of supernatural truth; the second is to send some one else to help me; the third is to help me Himself. If He has not adopted the first, then He must have chosen one of the other two. If He has not chosen the second, then there is no escape for me; for He must have adopted the third.

First: He could take me temporarily out of this Temple of Nature, give me such new senses as would put me *en rapport* with the invisible facts and phenomena of grace and the supernatural, leave me to ascertain of myself their laws just as I ascertain here the laws of nature; and then, when I am equipped with the knowledge of the truth, put me back into this Temple and leave me here to live aright and to die aright. But I know He has not done this. Therefore He must have adopted one of the two other only thinkable ways. If, then, He has not enabled me to help myself, He must, secondly, have sent some one else to help me; or, thirdly, He must have helped me by breaking through the dome of Nature, coming in to me Himself, and so placing Himself *en rapport* with me as to communicate with me intelligibly to myself.

Here, then, our pathway forks. And here, at this point, you are face to face with your first great question. How will you decide it? Which way will you take as you go on? To the left or straight ahead? If you decide that He sent some one else, you are a Unitarian. If you decide that He came Himself, you are a Trinitarian.

Indeed, there are independent reasons why God must be Triune. For the Divine Being must necessarily have the highest object of blissful contemplation, the highest means of happiness, or He would not be supremely happy. But God is Himself the highest of Beings. All creation is, of course, inferior to Him, and cannot therefore in itself furnish Him with such highest and most blissful contemplation. Such highest object of blissful contemplation must therefore be found, no otherwhere than in the archetypal structure Itself of God. Now an object of contemplation must be different from, it must be, in some sense, external to that which contemplates it. But how can there be in the *internal* structure of God an *external* object of contemplation? Only if God has existed from all past eternity in a Tri-unity, whereby the Father can behold His own blissful perfections as existing in and reflected from the Son, Who is Personally, though not in Substance, external to Himself; and the Son, those same objects of blissful contemplation reflected in the Holy Ghost; and the Holy Ghost can gaze upon His own perfections as they reside in the Father. The Trinity of Persons in the One Substance of God is what alone enables the Divine Being to find within Himself a divine Sabbath of active self-contemplation in supremest bliss from all past eternity; and this, because that which causes the consummation of bliss, viz.: the infinite perfection of love, joy and peace, is found within God, and not within creation, and mutually reflected within Him from Eternal Person to Eternal Person.

There are those who assert that it is impossible for a human mind of any strength to believe in the Tri-unity of God. But Plato, who possessed one of the profoundest, if not the profoundest uninspired mind that ever existed, did not think thus. He declared that the more deeply one thought of the Divine Being the more one found it impossible to conceive of Him as a strict Unit. It were certainly modest in us all to think just as deeply as did Plato, before we assert that the Tri-unity of God is something that a thoughtful man cannot hold.

Plato argues that, as creation has not had an eternal existence in the past, as there must, therefore, have been a time when God alone existed, it is impossible for the human mind, in contemplating the Divine Being as existing prior to and without any creation, to conceive of Him as a strict Unit. For if He had been a simple Unit, there having been, before creation, nothing external to such unit to awaken its attention as an object of contemplation, such unit could never have aroused out of its inactivity and non-self-consciousness to have produced creation at all. Therefore there must have been from all past eternity within God's Archetypal Structure Itself, in some way, exterior objects of Divine Contemplation; and the human mind is forced to admit the necessity of a species of Plurality within the Unity of God.

It is most remarkable, that Plato asserts that this

Plurality must be a Triplicity. The names which he gives to the three Principles are singularly in harmony with those which were subsequently fully revealed in Holy Scripture. To the first of his conceptions he applies the name 'Ἀγάπη, which means Love; to the second he gives the name Νοῦς, which means Intelligence; and to the third the title of life, Ψυχή.

However, I am not here addressing Unitarians. I am addressing those whose God is not the god of Mohammed. It was long since decided, and admirably set forth by the great French Dominican, that there are only three possible religions, viz.: one, whose statement is, "Man is God;" a second, whose statement is, "God is God;" and a third, whose statement is, "God is Man." The first is the religion of Polytheism; the second is the religion of Mohammedanism; the third is Christianity. Christianity declares that God has become Man, and so communicates with us directly. Mohammedanism says, this is impossible; God remains and is only God, and His communication with man is only through a prophet—through a second cause, through a creature. This also is the fundamental statement of Unitarianism; therefore Unitarianism is a European variety of the second form of religion, or Mohammedanism, agree ing with it in its mighty fundamental statement, " God is God," but simply varying that mighty statement into "Allah il Allah, and Christ is His prophet." But I am addressing, I say, those whose God is the God of St. John, of St. Augustine, of Luther, of Cranmer and of Wesley. It is unnecessary, therefore, for me to enter fully into the question whether, in helping us, God sent some one else. It is only necessary to say that if He sent some one else, then He has made the mistake of attempting to help us out of our conjectures, and failing to do so. For it is a patent fact that the Unitarians, acting on this supposition, are left conjecturing as to what is Truth? and what is God? and what are His ways? and what is Christ? as badly as ever. Semi-Arians against the Arians, Arians against the Socinians, Channing against Parker, Bellows against Frothingham. As, therefore, on the theory that some one else was sent, we are plunged into the absurdity of supposing that an all-powerful and all-perfect God of Love tried and failed to help us, that a perfect God is, therefore, imperfect, and a loving God either incompetent or unloving, we are forced to reject the second of the three ways of helping us.

There is but one more thinkable way. He must, then, have adopted that. There is no escape for us;

we must move straight along our path with the settled and permanent conclusion that God broke through the dome of Nature and came in among us Himself.

I am not only driven helplessly to this conclusion, gentlemen, by logic, by the absolute necessities of my case, and by the attributes of God, but I am confirmed in it, moreover, by the fact that here before me, in this very Temple of Nature, there is an extraordinary Book, which, whatever I may say of it, I know as a historic fact, foretold, long before the extraordinary Being came Whom they call the God-man, that, sooner or later, no less than God should come, as the desire of all nations, and be "with us," that He should be born of a virgin, and that His name should be called Wonderful, Counsellor, The Mighty God, The Everlasting Father, The Prince of Peace.

It must be God, too, for I must have nothing less than certainty as to supernatural truth and the laws of His grace. And certainty demands infallibility. All creatures, even the highest, are finite; they fall short of omniscience itself. For if the being be less than omniscient he may innocently lead me astray through ignorance. I am driven helplessly to admit, then, that God has come to help us.

I pass on, then; but, lo, I come suddenly to a spot

where the path forks again. We must pause again. Gentlemen, you are brought here face to face with your second great question. For God, having once come in a visible form, having so come that He can be touched by us, and can speak to us audibly through an organic form of human matter, one of two things must have happened subsequently. There are only two things possible to have happened; only two things thinkable. They are these, namely: He must either have so gone away again as not afterward to be visible, tangible and audible through a one organic form of humanity on earth, or He must have remained with us, visible, tangible and audible through a one organic form of humanity on earth. There is no *tertium quid*. There is your second great question. If you decide for the first alternative, then you are a Protestant. If you decide for the second, that God has still remained, and will to the end of time remain, in a one, undying, ever-fresh, amazing, organic, visible, audible, tangible and recognizable body of human matter, known as the Body Mystical of God on earth, out into which His Body Natural has without break or fissure expanded, then you are a Catholic. Whether you are of the Anglican, Roman or Greek part is a subsequent question; but you are a Catholic.

What is the relationship, then, between Protestantism and Catholicity? As we stand herewhere the path forks a second time, shall we take off to the left into theProtestant by-path, or shall we go straight on? Let us see.

"Oh, yes," says Protestantism; "God came 1,800 years ago to place Himself physically *en rapport* with us; He stayed thirty-three years; and then He went away, and is no longer on earth, visible and tangible in any one organic speaking body of human matter. But when He thus went away He left behind Him, for our certainty in matters of doctrinal truth, grace and salvation, a Book. Behold this, our sublime Bible. It is with this that we are *en rapport* since He left; and then He sends His influence from heaven, which in some recondite, spiritual and transcendental sense, helps each of us to find the truth as we apply ourselves to this, His precious legacy."

Certainly, I reply, this is an intelligible theory, and commands my respect. But I am to decide which way I am to go. Permit me to ask of you, then, What is the supernatural truth touching punishment hereafter? "Some of us who accept the 'Bible only,' claim that it is eternal, and others hold that it is not." Touching the necessity of Baptism and the Sacraments generally? "Some of us hold that they are necessary, and others that they are quite unnecessary." Touching the number of the Sacraments? 'Well, some of us claim that they are ordinances only, and not Sacraments at all; so that some claim that out of the seven there are only two, and others that there are none at all." Touching the atoning Cross? "Some of us claim that Its effect was universal; others that Its effect was particular only." But, touching Its necessity for salvation at all? "Well, some of us that accept the 'Bible only' claim that It is necessary, and others that It is not." Touching the necessity of a good life? "Well, there are some that claim it to be necessary to have wrought at least one hour, from the eleventh to the twelfth, for the penny of eternal life; others that the work of salvation is all completed if one, as the clock of life is striking twelve, utters the all-powerful and magical sentence 'I apprehend the Cross.'" Touching hereafter? "Some claim that there is only an eternal Heaven and an eternal Hell; others that besides these there is an intermediate temporal state of waiting; and still others, that there is no Hell at all." Touching Satan? "Some of us think there is such a being, others deny it." Touching God Himself? "Well, we are not agreed; some of us that accept the 'Bible only' hold that God is a Trinity; others, that The Father alone is God,'" and so on to the end of the chapter.

But if God came and thus went away and left only a Book and a vague influence, I do not see, O Protestantism, that we are very much helped. I do not see that we are not all still drowning in an ocean of mere conjecture as to what that Book says. I do not see that we are not all left still conjecturing touching the mightiest and most vastly important facts, phenomena and laws of grace and salvation;—God, who He is; man, and what his state is; hereafter; here, and the supernatural generally. Nay, your Book, with which alone you say you have been left, hath only stimulated conjecture concerning these things a thousand-fold. Before, we knew it was all guesswork; now you are all busy at guesswork, and do not realize it. This is the worst of all. For before, we faced conjecture, and knew what we faced—it was conjecture, unreliable, unverifiable. Now you face mere conjecture, and are all and severally cheating your selves into thinking, each his own is not conjecture at all.

By your theory, O Protestantism, a loving God flew to a world that was drowning in an ocean of conjecture, gave it a great hope of rescue, and then fled, leaving that behind Him which only hurled them back into a vaster, blacker and more tempestuous ocean of conjecture than ever. By your theory, O Protestantism, a loving God has done Satan's work! By your theory an omnipotent God has risen from His Throne to strive to do a work, and could not! By your theory an allwise and perfect God has devised and executed a plan, which has miserably failed amid the laughter of Hell! Your recondite, spiritual, transcendental, vague influence from Heaven, to guide you into certain Truth—what has come of it?

I love you, O my relatives! I respect your sacred memories, O my forefathers! but your Protestant bypath, and the dark and inextricable swamps into which it leads—it is no way for me to tread. I must bid you farewell and go on to the uplands of Truth. Venerable is the past, but venerable are not its errors They tell us that mediævalism is dead beyond resurrection. So it is. But the sixteenth century is just as dead, too. Begone, sheeted and stinking corpse! The nineteenth century hath come. We will live with the living, and not in tombs.

Gentlemen, I have led you up to the presence of your second great question. It was this: God having come in a visible form, must have done one of two only things: either have departed or remained; and remained, too, not in the vague, spiritual, transcendental sense of a mere impalpable influence—for that, we see, is practically to have departed—but remained in a real, tangible, visible and organic form, through which He can and does speak audibly to the world. These are the only thinkable alternatives. If He departed and left a book only, then we are Protestants. If He remained, "God with us," then we are Catholics. But we cannot adopt this position that He departed bodily without being driven by logic to deny our fundamental statement that God is a perfect, all-powerful and loving God; without being driven to the position that He is a God who strove to do what He could not; a God devising a plan that failed; a God wishing to help us, but powerless; a loving God giving us a hope but cheating us, and leaving us worse off than before. We are driven helplessly, then, on to the other alternative, namely, that having come in a speaking body of human matter, He remains in a speaking body, an organic form of human matter. And we find this one organic form, the human part of the God-man to-day on earth, in His Body Mystical, out into which His Body Natural of Palestine has, without break or fissure, gradually expanded over the earth, as human beings, plucked like branches from the root of the first Adam, have, out of all generations, been grafted into unity with It by Baptism, and as His one Body and Blood, passing through the Eucharist equally into all the branches, have incorporated them into Himself.

He is still the God-man on earth. He perpetually incarnates Himself. He is still "with us," taking human nature to Himself, and so abiding in a one visible Form of matter. That Form is the Catholic Church. It is not a mere society of men; it is the one organic Body Mystical of Christ. By It and through It, and Its marvelous arms and limbs, He literally touches us that His graces may flow through His touch. In It as Its living soul, and through It, He speaks to us audibly, that we may be certified we have the truth.

We are not cheated. We still have, by logic, by the necessities of our case, by the sanction of the Divine attributes, and in actual, historic and present existence, the Omniscient God on earth, remaining among us, according to the promise He made at a moment when, otherwise, we would have thought He was departing—"Lo, I am with you always, even unto the end of the world." In Him, in this God embodied in the one Church, in this God continuously visible and audible, therefore, behold, gentlemen, the Fountain of infallibility which you seek ; for God Himself cannot err nor falsify. And as the one Holy Catholic Church in all Its parts, His own Body, raises Its voice and chants in unison round and round the world, in unbroken strain, following the tireless sun through the centuries and the millenniums, the solemn Catholic Creed of Nice, Constantinople, and Athanasius, listen : it is the voice of God on earth, Who chanted the great prophetic psalm, "Deus, Deus," from the Cross, chanting aloud that all the peoples in all time may hear, and be without excuse, the unaltering irre formable Truth.

SECOND CONFERENCE.

CATHOLICITY, A LIFE AND AN ORGANIZER; PROTESTANTISM, A DISORGANIZER AND A DEATH.

GENTLEMEN,

St. Thomas of Aquinas defines Life as a spontaneous motion. It is something more than this. It is a mysterious principle pervading the universe, which possesses a centralizing force. It organizes and harmonizes. It sustains in existence the organic form which it has constructed. It is the mother of order and beauty. It builds the crystalline forms with their glittering angles; it works out for itself, and then produces the rustic tracery of the tree; it frames and holds together the bird, the beast and man; it constructs the family, the State, the Church; its fountain is God, and its sanction is, "Thou shalt do no murder." On the other hand, Death is a disorganizer. It is a despoiler of beauty. On its anvil it smites the diamond into powder; it lays the tree low; it slays bird and beast and man; it sends hate, divorce and orphanage into the family, feuds into the State, schism into the Church; its fountain is in hell, and its fiat is:

"That which is, shall not be; that which is gathering into unity, shall be scattered into severalty; that which is organizing, shall be decomposed." Life, then, is the love of beauty and of order; Death their foe and destroyer.

It is my privilege, gentlemen, at this conference to present Catholicity to you as a Life and as an Organizer; and it will follow that the fountain whence She springs is God, and not Satan.

What was it that this life, issuing from the bosom of God, went forth to organize and to compact? What was it that was to be gathered together out of its severalty into unity? It was the human race; which, when it fell away from God, went into pieces, and lay upon earth disintegrated and dying. It fell from Him Who was not only the Life, but Who was also Love. Cut off from Charity, therefore, selfishness, hates, envies and angers were the mutually repellant force in its bosom, sundering its individuals apart from each other, its families and its States.

The life, which we call Catholicity, goes forth into these ruins as an organizing and integrating force to build a structure of order and beauty. What was its cohesive operation as it thus went forth; and what the marvelous structure it erects and sustains? It formed an organism in which are four great couplings or unifications. The first of these unifications had, indeed, existed in the eternity of the past—namely, the unity of the Father and the Son in the archetypal, interior structure of God ; the second and the third of the great couplings take place during the scene of time present ; in order to carry the fourth, final and permanent unity, namely, of human beings with Christ, through the eternity of the future. Go back with me, then, to the first, and behold this living force of Catholicity going forth to its great integrating, organizing and centralizing work among the poor fragments with which it has to deal. Behold the unifications which it successively effects as it proceeds in its benign work.

1st. From all past eternity the Father and the Son in God have been of One Substance. If the Father is God, the Son is God of God ; if the Father is Light, the Son is Light out of Light ; and as the Father is Life, the Son is Life of Life : *i. e.* life flows out of the Father, Who is its fountain in God, and owing to the unity between the Father and the Son so fills the Son that the Son can come to the earth with the great statement, " I am the Life." Here, then, we have the first unification ; in God from all past eternity the Father and the Son are One. It is in the Trinity and the entire unity of Its Persons that we have the hope and the prophecy of human reintegration. For, secondly, God the Son descended into the Temple of Nature, took manhood to Himself in the womb of the Virgin, was born and stood among us the God-man. Here we have the second great unification effected; Christ's Manhood, namely, so entirely one with His Godhead, that there was no obstruction to hinder the life, which from all past eternity He had from the Father, from flowing from His Godhead into and filling His Manhood.

3d. The third great unity in the successive steps was the oneness between Christ's Man's Nature and His Church; a union, as we saw at our last conference, without break or fissure between them. Indeed, Scripture exhausts all metaphor in the effort to make us realize the consummate integrity of this third great unification. The oneness of man and wife, though they be declared by God to be one only flesh, is not sufficient. The oneness of the head and human body, though "from the head all the body is by joints and bands knit together," is not sufficient. If we are the branches, He is not the stock, but the whole vine. Indeed, the Church is so one with Him that it is called by His name, Jesus Christ. Owing, therefore, to the unity between the Man's Nature of Christ and His Church, the life which had flowed from His Godhead into His Body Natural now flows out from the latter and fills His Church.

4th. There is but one more unification, the fourth, which completes the vast constructive work. In it the poor broken fragments are reintegrated into this structure, organized, harmonized and sustained: namely, the unity effected by the Holy Ghost in Baptism between each separated individual of the race and this one Catholic Church. The life therefore that is in the Church, now flows into the baptized man owing to his unity with the Church.

Behold, then, gentlemen, the kindly, loving, reconstructive force of Catholic life at its work, gathering poor disintegrated humanity, one by one, through the fourth unification into oneness with its one Holy Catholic and Apostolic Church—which was already one with the Manhood of Christ; which Manhood was, through the second unification, already one with the Godhead of Christ; which Godhead, through the first unification, was always one with God the Father in the eternity of the past. Behold how life, flowing with a unity of purpose through these living links, binds all together—Christians, Church, Christ and the Father

Who is the Fountain of Life—into a unique and sublime structure, and carries reintegrated humanity out of time present to sustain it in God through the eternity of the future. Behold, too, in all this, how the one Holy Catholic Church and Its Baptismal Sacrament are inseparable, indispensable and undying elements in the whole grand organism of life and unity. "Thou shalt not commit murder," is the sanction of the sacredness and pricelessness of that one visible Apostolic Church, and of its blessed life-giving Sacraments. To slay the Godhead of Christ and the Trinity and the Incarnation as do the Arians, Socinus and Priestly; to slay the Church as does Protestantism; to slay the Sacraments as do Simeon and Chillingworth, is to break in upon this structure of unity, and to slay God's plan of salvation.

But, gentlemen, in all this, what have I been giving you? I have simply been giving you that plan of salvation, that Gospel in little, that solemn Creed of Nice, Constantinople and Athanasius, which the three Communions, Anglican, Roman and Greek, of the One Catholic Church, which the three national types of Catholic man, Saxon, Latin and Oriental, hold in common. and chant ceaselessly to the peoples as the sun goes round the world through the centuries; the

Christian Creed, which that one tripartite Holy Catholic Church alone, too, holds. For Protestantism, which is the disintegrating, destructive, disorganizing and scattering element in Christianity, does not and cannot hold that Creed, or proclaim it to the nations. Do you ask why? Two reasons. Following its death-giving instincts, it rends that Creed apart, disintegrating it article from article, and then cheats the world by declaring of each and every separate article, "I believe it." But the Creed, like all of Catholicity's works, is organic and a unit; it is built up, a thing of life like a flower; article grows out of previous article, and opens out into the following; so that its articles cannot thus be sundered from each other, or re-arranged, any more than a flower can be torn apart, petal from petal, and sepal from stamen, and pistil from ovary, and remain a flower. Though you may have in your hand afterward all its parts, you have not the flower. For this holy and unalterable Creed of Catholicity expresses something as a whole, over and above the sense of its separate articles, which is the very thing, the very Gospel, the very plan of salvation Protestantism will not admit, hates, and with murderous instinct would slay. It makes necessary the four great unifications, and among them, as a part of the plan of salvation, the one great Catholic Church in Its Saxon, Oriental and Latin sides ; Its Apostolic ministry, and Its Sacrificial, Sacerdotal and Sacramental systems.

Secondly : but I hear you say, gentlemen, surely Protestantism asserts that it believes in a Catholic Church. True ; but what does it mean? It means, and it means avowedly, merely some vague, disintegrated nebula of all tolerably good folk, baptized and unbaptized, for it includes the Quakers and others. Nebula, do I say? A nebula is something we can see, at least with a telescope, and map out in its general shape, however hazy. But this indiscriminate muster of Protestantism retires, when we look at it, into the complete indistinctness and incertitude of a profound and permanent invisibility. Gentlemen, this is not the organic Catholic Church of the Creed. This is not to believe the Creed, but to believe something else of Protestantism's own invention. To believe the Creed, is to believe what that Creed was written to mean, and what it always has meant from time immemorial. But to excogitate out of the profound depths of ingenuity a totally new and modern idea, and to cover that totally different and antagonistic idea with the garment of an ancient phrase, and then send the new idea forth, a mere wolf in sheep's clothing, is to act the part of the disingenuous, and tc do the work of him whom the Saviour called "the liar from the beginning and the father of lies." The phrase "Holy Catholic Church" is a cover of definite shape that will fit only one receptacle; and it cannot be made, by any manipulation, to hold under itself and within its rims the innumerable suppositions of Protestantism sprawling off hither and yon at their own wild will.

But life is not only an organizing and uniting force, it is also, as St. Thomas says, a spontaneous motion. Now "all motion," (I quote from another) "bears in its very essence the idea of a starting point, of a point to be reached. and of an effort to pass from the one to the other." If, then, Catholicity be a life and not a destroyer, if its fountain be in God and not in hell, then, as such life, it must exhibit not only this constructive force which I have shown, but also this element of motion, and these peculiarities of motion—namely, a starting point, a point to be reached, and a flowing from the one to the other.

High up in far-away mountains there is a vast reservoir of water. From the end of that great lake its floods tumble in white cataract into a basin on a lower level, and form there a second enormous reservoir. From the opposite end of this second lake the waters tumble again into a third basin on a still lower level. From the opposite end of this third basin they fall again into a fourth lake still further below. From the lower end of this fourth sheet of water they issue in innumerable radiating rills and streams over the level lowlands, filling them with verdure, with beauty and with fruits. You have here in these four lakes, one below the other, and the luxuriant plain spread out at their foot, an apt illustration of life and grace issuing as a motion from God the Father, and reaching at last by Mediation the lowlands of poor humanity, to turn them from a desert into a garden. Life and grace, which we all need in place of death and weakness, issue from God the Father, their original Fountain, and fall first into God the Son. They next fall into the Man's Nature of Jesus Christ. From this they descended on Pentecost into the great lake of the Catholic Church, filling its enormous basin; whence they issue finally and flow, through the openings of the Sacraments, into the many stream beds of human lives, and fill the world with the flowers of sanctity and the fruits of good works. God the Father is the starting point of this life. God the Son, in His

Catholic Church and through Its Sacraments, is the mediatory receptacle, from Whom this overflowing life and grace reach humanity, which is the term of all.

In our last conference I conducted you up to Jesus Christ in His visible Catholic Church as its Soul and Life. It was here that you found, embodied on earth, Him who is Infallibility itself, because He is God. It is through this, His one visible, organic Body Mystical, inseparable from Himself, unless indeed you slay the God-man now on earth, that you heard Him chanting continuously the unalterable and irreformable truth. And that in which He chants aloud this truth to all the nations is the Catholic Creed.

What, then, is the Creed? What is the infallible truth? In what I have said above, I repeat, I have been giving you simply that Catholic Creed. For the Creed is nothing less and nothing more than a history of the course which life and grace take from stage to stage, as they issue from God the Father, and, passing through the Godhead, and the Body Natural and Mystical of the Son, reach at last, through Baptism, human beings that need them. The Creed is the Gospel in little; the good news unto men; the way of salvation. For the Creed begins with: "*I believe in one God the Father Almighty, Maker of heaven and* earth, *And of all things visible and invisible.*" It begins, then, with the Father as the Fountain of all things ; the Fountain, therefore, of the life and grace which we need after the fall. But it is the history, not of all things, but simply of the course of that grace. It passes next, therefore, and announces the reservoir into which life and grace first flow from the Father: "*And in one Lord Jesus Christ the only begotten Son of God;*" and it announces the first unification ; that, namely, between Father and Son, existing in the eternity of the past: "*Begotten of His Father before all worlds, God of God; Light of Light; very God of very God; Begotten not made; Being of one substance with the Father; By Whom all things were made.*"

It then gives the next reservoir into which the life and grace flow, and announces the second great unification—namely, God and man in Christ—"*Who for us men, and for our salvation, came down from heaven, And was incarnate by the Holy Ghost of the Virgin Mary, And was made man.*" But human nature, before it could, even as it stood on earth in the person of Christ, receive and be filled with the very fullness of life and grace, must first undergo, even in Christ, a time of probation, of temptation, of trial. There are profound reasons for this, almost if not quite beyond the grasp of human ken, but which God Himself displays in furtive flashes out of that sublime passage beginning, "For it became Him for Whom are all things, and by Whom are all things, in bringing many sons to glory, to make the Captain of their salvation perfect through sufferings," and ending with, "For in that He, Himself, hath suffered, being tempted, He is able to succor them that are tempted." The Creed, therefore, goes on to give the process by which the Man's Nature of Christ was prepared through *"sufferings, crucifixion under Pontius Pilate, death and burial, to rise again the third day, and to ascend,*" not astronomically, but to ascend in the *highest moral and spiritual elevation, even into the condition and lofty spiritual companionship of the Most High,* "to receive there," in that moral and spiritual exaltation, "the gifts for men," and, on Pentecost, to pour those gifts forth from His Body Natural which had thus gained them, and fill with them His Body Mystical, the Church. Hence the Creed goes on to say, "*I believe in the Holy Ghost, the Lord and Giver of Life, Who proceedeth from the Father, and*" not from the Father only, but also from "*the Son ; and I believe in the one Holy Catholic and Apostolic Church.*"

Here we strike the third great unification—the oneness, nay, the identity of the Church with the Man's Nature of Christ, even as it is said, "The Church, which is His Body, the fullness of Him that filleth all in all;" and as it is said again, "Ye are the Body of Christ and members in particular." Let us pause here a moment before we go on to the conclusion of the Creed.

You will remember that at the close of our last conference we were left forced into a certain conclusion. We were forced by logic, by the necessities of our case, and by the attributes of God Himself, into the conclusion that God, having descended visibly into the Temple of Nature, having so come that He could touch and be touched by us, and that He could speak to us audibly through an organic form of human matter, must have remained with us in a one visible form of human matter. This kind of remaining only, we found, would be an effectual relief. The other only thinkable suppositions left us worse off than ever. Besides, why should one small country, one brief generation, thus have the inestimable boon of His presence *en rapport* with itself, and not all nations and all subsequent time as well? Let us take up this subject, then, where we left it at the last conference, particularly as it relates to the spot in the Creed at which we have arrived.

We having been forced into the conclusion that God must remain on earth *en rapport* with us, the problem here is, How was He thus to remain in a one organic body of human matter; a continuous body, too, that should be His own Body, still surrounding His Soul and Divinity, and in unbroken unity with Them? There are many reasons why, if the first or natural form of His Body had continued visible among us, it would not have satisfied the requirements of our case. For that first form and condition of His visible Body was loca.; it could stand on only one contracted spot, while we need Him simultaneously in all nations, all round the world, in a Body that shall speak to us, forgive us our sins, touch us and feed us. To that first condition of His visible Body, which we call the Body Natural, a few thousand only could have clustered at one time; while we all, and all round the world, need to gather simultaneously to "God with us," at any time and at all times. The overwhelming majority of the human race, moreover, are sons of toil, and could not have traveled to Him. Besides, there were something shocking in the supposition of that fair form upon whose bosom St. John leaned, continuing visible for centuries, descending to the wrinkled brow and thin silver locks of extreme old age, and lasting, undying, beyond even that, in a decrepitude of millenniums which we know nothing of. This were the extreme of the unnatural. God never acts in a shocking or unnatural way; and such act were beneath the dignity of God. And yet logic, our necessities and the attributes of God have driven us to the only conclusion that God must remain on earth in His one organic Body; that He must so remain as not to shock us; that He must so remain that His Body shall be, however aged, yet ever fresh and youthful; ever one, yet everywhere simultaneously present throughout the world. Mighty problem! Who shall solve it? Not you, gentlemen, nor I, nor the wisest philosopher that ever lived. But what is thus beyond human ingenuity—what is quite impossible to men—is easy to God. For there are natural laws of growth and expansion, and there are supernatural laws of growth and expansion. The Divine voice had said in the ancient time that "The stone cut out without hands," the Human, visible Nature of Christ, should "grow and become a great mountain and fill the whole earth." And the Divine ingenuity, in the fullness of time, found out a way by which His Body Natural could expand without break or fissure into His Body Mystical, the Catholic Church, and fill the whole earth. The Natural and the Mystical forms of His Body of human matter are but two consecutive visible conditions of that Body; the one local, the other universal; its natural condition going up and disappearing on Olivet, only that the Mystical condition might thenceforward alone be visible and tangible on earth. Natural bodies expand from infancy to childhood, to youth, to manhood, by natural law; God's Human Body then continued ceaselessly to expand, but by supernatural law. Besides, at the very time when we would have supposed that, on Olivet, He was departing out of his condition of visibility among us, He took occasion solemnly to disabuse us of this error; to disclose to us that He was not; to say to us, "Lo, I am still with you, even unto the end of the world." Of course He had always been with us in His impalpable omnipresence. If He had meant to say that He would merely continue thus to be invisibly and inaudibly with us, a mere influence, He would have been uttering a needless truism. Nay, it was no such truism that He was guilty of. But what He impressed upon us was that, as He had been *en rapport* with us, so He would continue to be until the end. The event at Olivet was a disappearance of the first and temporary condition of his visibility to make way for the second and lasting condition. He that first took our human nature, binding it to Himself in the womb of the Virgin, goes on taking our human nature to Himself till the number of the elect is made up. The Incarnation is a perpetual fact. What is the supernatural law, then, under which His own Personal Body continues to expand? It is this: human beings are baptized into Christ, according as it is said, "We are members of His body, of His flesh and of His bones.'" Human beings, sprouting like so many separate branches from the poisoned root of Adam, are plucked thence by the Holy Ghost, and, in Baptism, grafted into the new tree, Christ; our bodies into His, our souls into His, our hopes, our imaginations, our passions, our reason into His; and so the Tree enlarges; so His Body visible expands; so "the Stone grows and becomes a great Mountain and fills the whole earth;" according as it is said, "Ye are the Body of Christ and members in particular." Branch after branch being thus grafted into the Vine, Christ then sends forth through the Eucharist His one Body and Blood into all the branches simultaneously, and binds them up together into His own visible Catholic Body; according as it is said, "For we being many, are one bread and one body, for we are all partakers of that one bread." And so, since the Resurrection and until the end of time, it is life that still playeth in His Body on earth. The Catholic life is among us ; the life that centralizes, organizes, integrates, harmonizes, beautifies, builds and sustains that Body. No, no ; death, that disorganizes, loosens and scatters, hath no part in It. It hath overcome death ; and, lo, "The gates of hell shall not prevail against It."

Life is not only thus, gentlemen, the love of order, and of organism, and of unity, but it is also the love of freshness and of beauty. God Himself, who is the Life, must by the laws of His Being finish His works. He must adorn the meadows with flowers, the streams with rocks and cascades, the lakes with green islands, each billow with a white blossom atop, and the very night with diamonds. And life from God could not enter into and play within the great Catholic Body, without Its breaking forth also, not only into the beauty of meekness and of purity and of all sanctity, but also into the wonders of fair religious statuary, paintings, architecture and music, the robed procession, the incense, the banner, the fringed canopy, the brilliant altar, and the fair pomp and form. It was that whose other name is Death, the destroyer, the foe of organism, of freshness and of beauty, that smote all this in the sixteenth century, and tramples the flowers to-day as the fecund Life sends them forth once more to clothe the wide waste of desolation.

Here, then, we have, gentlemen, the infallible God in a Body on earth, even in the One Holy Catholic and Apostolic Church, as its Soul. And because we say of a man that we see him when we look at his form, though his soul be invisible, so we all around the world, as they in Palestine, have the Infallible God still visible, tangible and audible among us; we see Him, we touch Him with reverent hand.

Now, His Body of human matter having thus grown out by supernatural law into so marvelous and everywhere present a structure, it follows, if He is to continue to apply Himself to the world through It, as He did in Palestine through His Natural Body, that It must have everywhere new and marvelous limbs and organs which He may stretch forth to poor humanity, and by which He may touch us, and teach us, and pardon us, and feed us. In Palestine, with the limbs of His Body Natural, He tenderly touched the white eye-balls of the blind and the silent ear-chambers of the deaf He laid His loving hands on children, on the sick, on the sinner, and on bread and wine, that pardon, and blessing, and transformation, and all gifts and graces might flow from Him through His Body, and through even His garments, to those that were touched. What, then, are the new and marvelous limbs of this His marvelous supernatural Body? They are the Catholic, life-giving, grace-conferring Sacraments and Ministry. These are but limbs of His Personal Body Mystical, which He stretches forth to us, by which He touches us, and conveys to us His graces all around the world.

A hand and arm separated from a living human body is but a piece of powerless clay. But slip the arm into its socket in the living body, and the soul within, using that poor piece of clay, performs with it its own mighty deeds. So a man separated from Christ's Body Mystical—a man considered merely in himself alone—is the very type of powerlessness. But when set in a socket of Christ's Mystical Body as a Priest or a Bishop, the God within that Body, using the poor frame of clay as His own arm and hand, performs with it His divine and mighty deeds among us. pardons in the Sacrament of Penitence, transforms bread and wine at the Altar, blesses, regenerates in Baptism, anoints with the Holy Ghost in Confirmation, makes of twain one flesh, confers the grace of Orders through His touch, and either raises the sick from death or sends the soul healed into eternity. The Sacraments and the Ministry are His limbs with which He touches us. Tactual succession? Why of course " God is with us " in a Body, and literally touches us. When His arm and hand, a Priest, baptises an infant, it is not a man that is baptising, or mere water that we are looking at; we are looking at Christ's own arm and hand stretched forth and visibly taking our dear one and grafting it into Himself; at the holy Altar we see in the human Priest God's visible hand touch and bless the bread before our eyes and convey it to us; when one is confirmed or ordained to the Priesthood we are literally beholding Christ stretching forth His marvelous hand, a Bishop, and conveying the Holy Ghost either to the work of the ordinary Christian or to the work of the Priesthood. And it is He that at last takes our poor soulless body and, in the requiem, lays it tenderly away till He shall summon it at the resurrection. Beware; he that hath eyes to see let him see. The quickening touch of God's Body on earth? Ah, gentlemen, as true are the words of Manning, as they are consummately beautiful: " When the Wisdom of God came into the world, He laid His hands upon a multitude of things; upon the sick, the afflicted, the hungry, the dying; upon little children, upon the bread He blessed and brake in the wilderness; upon sorrow and upon pain; and, lastly, He laid them upon the Cross; and wherever He laid His hands He left a sweetness and a fragrance which wisdom can perceive and wisdom alone can know." Look, gentlemen, at your Protestantism. O Protestantism, in thine unwisdom thou wilt drag the world, and even the little ones of thy bosom, away from the touch of Christ.

Here, then, stands the Catholic Church with continuous life from the first; here It stands all round the world. In It is God, for It is His personal Body; through It He applies Himself by Ministry and Sacraments to poor humanity; to It He made the solemn promise that He would guide It, when It spoke as a unit, into all truth; not that It could possibly speak error any more than could His Body Natural in Palestine, It being the organ of His Soul and Divinity; but He made the solemn promise in kindly and descending consideration to our weakness. If He promised to guide It, when It spoke as a unit, into all truth, how can any one suppose it to be fallible, and liable to lead us into error, without charging Christ with breaking His promise, and so not being

God at all? Thus it is always that the Protestant denial of the infallibility of the Catholic Church is a first fatal step in that inevitable logical descent, which ends in denying the Godhead of Christ and setting up Unitarianism with its murder of the Atonement in the world.

What, then, has the Catholic Church, as a unit, spoken? What is the infallible Truth? It is the Creed which I have given you. This is all that It has formally announced by Its six general Councils. This is the antagonist of Protestantism, since life is always the antagonist of death. But, besides the formal statements of the Creed, there are other things which we know to be true also; not because the whole Church Catholic hath formulated them in general Council and accepted them as thus formulated, but because the Church's documentary voice has always, and in all Its three parts, everywhere declared them, and would have thrown them into formulæ had it been necessary; viz., the Sacerdotal and Sacramental systems, the Apostolic succession, Priestly absolution, the real objective presence of Christ in the Eucharist, Baptismal regeneration, Prayers for the dead, and lights, incense, vestments, adoration and song as the five essentials of Christian worship. Of these all, every part of the Catholic Church, ancient, mediæval and modern, Latin, Saxon and Oriental, Anglican, Roman and Greek, have held no doubt, but have continuously and consentingly asserted them in ritual and official documents. The points on which the Anglican, Greek and Roman Communions differ are points over and above these; points upon which the whole Church has not yet spoken.

Let us return and go on with the Creed. After making its great announcement, "*I believe in the one Holy Catholic and Apostolic Church*," it proceeds to announce the fourth and final great unification in the reconstructing work that Life is effecting—namely, "*I acknowledge one Baptism for the remission of sins.*" In this Baptism each individual is brought into unity with the reservoir of grace. And then comes the grand close. For, of course, there follows from the internal life-action of this great organic Catholic Structure, "*The communion of all the saints*" within It. Furthermore, as death is only by sin, there follows from the cure of sin the cure of death. The Creed's next article is, therefore, "*I look for the resurrection of the dead.*" What, finally, is the end and purport of all this flow of grace and life, and of all these four unifications? What is the final result of al' this integrating, organizing, centralizing, harmonizing and sustaining force of Catholic life as it goes forth from God to broken humanity? It is salvation. Therefore the Creed rounds out and completes its history with the final statement, "*And the life everlasting in the world to come. Amen.*" Thus is the Creed a consecutive history of Life as a motion, of Life as a redintegrator, organizer, harmonizer and sustainer—of Catholic Life, the foe of death, with which the race was struck at the Fall.

In the wonderful land of the West there are two processes going on simultaneously, the one on the lowlands, the other on the uplands. In the serene and sunny valleys of Sonoma and Suisun, of Santa Clara, Los Angeles and Sacramento, those paradises on earth, the vine dresser, the florist and the agriculturist ply their peaceful, kindly crafts; healing all abrasions in the soil, terracing rugged slopes, gathering out unsightly stones, and covering everywhere with verdure and billowy beauty. But high up on the sides of the Sierra there is a different work and a different scene. There, it is the miner that has left his record. With his sluice-heads and the tremendous impact of their out-bounding water-spouts he has turned up the mountain sides for miles; turf and flower and rounded mound fly to pieces before him; he strips away the soil from the land; he turns the streams from their own sweet ways of mystery; he disembowels the hills; he decomposes them, throwing up great mounds of boulders, and spreading wide expanses of sand in his exploiture of the gold. And he has left behind him, wherever he has trodden, one vast, broken, verdureless scene of desolation and death, which it will take kindly nature centuries to heal, to cure and to cover. One cannot help standing in admiration before this daring and this power of our human nature. Its work on the slopes of the Sierra is, indeed, a mighty work. But, gentlemen, it is a ghastly work.

The instinct of Protestantism is the instinct, alas, of disruption, disintegration and death. Leaping upon Jesus Christ, it hath rent His Body Mystical, the Church, apart from His Body Natural of Palestine, and sent Him, with His Body Natural, into a far-away astronomic heaven. Leaping, then, upon the Body Mystical, the Catholic and Apostolic Church on earth, it hath disconnected Its outward and visible from Its inward part; and, while it lauds its disembodied "Church invisible and spiritual," buries the dead visible part as some offensive thing, fit only to be put out of sight. Leaping upon Christendom, it lacerates it into numerous fighting sects, and, alas, glories in its disorganizing work, as producing a beautiful and actively writhing variety. Leaping upon the rounded perfect number of the seven Sacraments, it slays five outright; and, instantly springing upon each of the other two, it tears its soul from its body; Baptism is left without the divine regenerating force of life, the Eucharist is despoiled of its tremendous, adorable Freight, and is left a mere natural and lifeless piece of bread and a memory of the natural man. Leaping upon man as an *immortal* being, it disjoins body from soul, and, ignoring the former, appeals only to the latter with, "Save your soul; oh, save your soul." But, O Jesus, Thou didst tell us to fear him who is able to destroy both body and soul in hell. Leaping upon man as a *worshiping* being, it sunders body from soul, and forbids the worship of the body—no fasting, no reverent bending of the head on entering God's presence in God's House, or at the Sacred Names, as little kneeling and as little standing as possible. But, O Jesus, Thou hast taught us that the body is a creature of God as well as the soul ; and Thou hast taught us to worship the Lord our God ; and to pray that " both our hearts and bodies may be directed, sanctified, and governed in the ways of this Thy law, and in the works of this Thy commandment." O Jesus, Thou hast taught us, too, that we are to worship Thee in spirit and in truth. And how can we worship Thee in truth if our body play not with our spirit in its changing moods of glorious praise, of lowly humility and of reverent adoration; how can we worship Thee in truth if our body belie the moods of the spirit? O Jesus, Thou hast taught us, too, that our body is grafted into Thine; that it is precious to Thee, too, as it is to the very instincts Thou hast planted in us; and that Thou wilt rescue it from death. And Thou hast taught us to pray, " that, through Thy most mighty protection, we may be preserved both here and ever in body and in soul." Nay, cries Protestantism, we have decomposed the man, and the body is dead as a worshiper. Not satisfied with slaying the Body Mystical, it has cut the Church asunder, not only longitudinally, but also transversely. For it has sundered Church Militant here from Church Expectant and Triumphant there, hurling the beloved departed so far away, that the gulf between the living and the dead is bridgeless, that all communication is gone, and that neither can give the other the charity of its prayers. O God upon Thy Throne, must not even Thine heart have been filled with amazement as, to

Thy listening ear, the voice of Thy needy children's prayers for each other died away into silence! It decomposes the organic Christian Creed, and holds out in its hand the poor *disjecta membra* of the once fair flower, that the world may admire its death. It lays hands on the ancient Apostolic three-fold Ministry, slays the Bishop and the Deacon, and, at last, leaves the world without even a Priest.

While the Anglican rubrics, as all other Catholic rubrics, speak of but one Priest, of but one Celebrant at each Eucharist, and of but one Officiant at each Morning or Evening Prayer, thereby symbolizing the truth that there is but one great Priest, Jesus Christ, and that it is heresy to divide Him (one Celebrant, I say, who may be assisted, indeed, in epistle and gospel, and one Officiant, who may be assisted in the Lessons), it has with its disruptive force, as the foe of unity, invaded our own Church, and sundered the Officiant's and the Celebrant's part of the service into halves, or into more numerous fragments still, and has parceled them out to various Officiants, breaking up even this symbol of the Oneness of Christ. While the rubrics say the services shall be musically rendered, thus securing the unity of the worship as a symbol of the unity of the parish and of the Church which worships with one voice, it has, with its instinct of disruption, gone down into our congregations, disintegrated this mode of unison in rendering the service, and separated it into a broken mumble of voices.

With boisterous might it has divided religion from æsthetics, and has then proceeded to deprave architecture and to trample ecclesiastical fine arts under its feet. It has debased manners, until the "gentleman of the old school" is a phrase descriptive of a culture and a suavity that are well-nigh gone. It has gone down beneath with its besom to sweep hell away; nay, in its Unitarian form, it has even mounted to the Throne of God Himself, and has there disintegrated and separated Father, Son and Holy Ghost from each other, slain the Holy Ghost, destroyed the Son, and left the Father without a Son, sterile and alone upon His throne.

Behold, then, gentlemen, Catholicity, a Life issuing from God; an organizing, centralizing, harmonizing, constructive and beautifying Force! And behold, too, Protestantism, the mother of uncomeliness, a disorganizing, decentralizing, disruptive and destroying power! One cannot but admire its might and its daring. Its work on the slopes of time is indeed a mighty work. But, gentlemen, it is a ghastly work.

THIRD CONFERENCE.

CATHOLIC CHURCH, PERFECT AND IMPERFECT. LEAVES ROOM FOR PLAY OF MENTAL ACTIVITY. CATHOLICITY THE "YEA" OF CHRISTIANITY; PROTESTANTISM THE "NAY." TRUE CAUSE OF PROTESTANT REFORMATION. PROTESTANTISM, DIVERSITY WITHOUT UNITY; ROME, UNITY WITHOUT DIVERSITY; CATHOLICITY, UNITY IN DIVERSITY.

CERTAIN attacks having been made by the pulpit and the press upon the author of these Conferences, subsequently to the delivery of the First and of the Second, he stepped out in front of the rostrum, and made the following remarks before beginning the Third Conference, viz.:

I have come up to the consideration of this topic not to attack a single human being living. I am, on the other hand, criticising a system. The whole issue is too solemn, too lofty, too vital in itself for either side so far to forget itself as to lose temper. I am attacking not Protestants, for I have many respected and many dearly loved friends and near relatives who are Protestants; but I am attacking Protestant*ism*. I am attacking not Roman Catholics, for I have loved and respected friends who are Roman

Catholics ; but I am attacking Roman*ism*. I speak, gentlemen, not at my own motion, but in obedience to your call. Hitherto, abstracts only of these Conferences have appeared in the secular press. Indeed who could expect that any daily paper could find space, in this busy age, for six long addresses, each four solid columns in length? But it results as a fact, that the public outside of this building cannot adequately ascertain the ideas of this counter-Reformation. Before me indeed is a great sea of heads ; but you, gentlemen, are nothing in comparison with the vast public. They cannot comprehend what it is that has banded together the 17,400 of the nobility, gentry and clergy of the "English Church Union," the 12,000 of the "Church of England Workingmen's Defense Association," the 14,000 members of the "Confraternity of the Blessed Sacrament," nor the thousands that signed the late monster petition to the authorities in England. And certainly the position of the Catholic school of thought cannot properly, nor indeed at all adequately, be answered, unless it is comprehended.

The *Tribune*, day before yesterday, very naturally, therefore, fell into the mistake of speaking of this great movement, which began more than a half century ago, as a retreat toward the Roman Church ; and Mr.

Beecher, in his two sermons on Sunday last, virtually gave the same impression. All this shows how radically the movement is misunderstood.

In a brief word, then, Catholics claim that Protestantism has failed *as a preservative of Christianity* on earth. The two main counts in the indictment presented ten years ago against Protestantism were, that if its premises were true, its logical conclusion was not Christianity but infidelity; that Theodore Parker and Frothingham were the legitimate brain-children of John Calvin and Martin Luther; and that it is impossible for any of the Trinitarian Protestant sects to answer Parker's and Frothingham's arguments. It seems amazing to me, that it should have become necessary to reiterate this. I thought I had stated it distinctly enough, even for prejudice to understand it. Secondly, that what ought thus logically to happen after three hundred years of Calvinism and Lutheranism, has happened historically—namely, that while Protestantism two or three hundred years ago held great thoughtful peoples, it has failed to retain its hold on those peoples; that with rare exceptions it has today lost both their intellect and their masses. Ten years ago, with all that was said in pulpit and press, these two counts in the indictment were in no one case met and answered. But ten years have begun to work a change. Robert Dale Owen, in his calmly written Introduction to "The Debatable Land," admits them, and says the time is passed for the Protestant ministers to close their eyes to the facts. Mr. Beecher last Sunday admits, and even more fully than your speaker had ever charged, that it is indeed true, that lands once believing the Protestant presentment of Christianity are to-day honey-combed with atheism, pantheism and infidelity generally. He says that skepticism is wide-spread in the pews even of the very Protestant churches themselves; that a photograph of what is going on in the brains of the people as the preachers preach would be curious; that sober-faced, thoughtful gentlemen sit in the pews, and listen, and say in reply in their minds, "'Maybe-Maybe,' which means 'No.'"

Ah, then, it is beginning to be admitted at last that Protestantism is effete. To say nothing of Noah's ark against which, by the way, the stubborn multitudes, who were shortly after drowned, protested most vigorously, I am afraid Mr. Beecher is about as wise in remaining in Protestantism, as I should be if I insisted on sailing to Albany in a sloop, or going to Boston in a stage-coach, instead of using the railroad or steamboat. Mr. Beecher's entire sermon condenses down to the following statement: "Yes, Protestantism has destroyed Christian belief and created infidels, pantheists and atheists by the thousands. And, isn't it glorious!" Mr. Beecher, Mr. Beecher, you shouldn't joke in the pulpit.

Now, this counter-Reformation of ours goes on to say, "Yes, and Romanism is a failure, too; the sixteenth century burst that bubble; and to-day Roman lands also are honey-combed with infidelity."

Is *Christianity* a failure, then? Why, it would be, were there no other presentment of Christianity than the Roman and the Protestant presentments. But there is a third presentment, radically different both from the Roman and from the Protestant. And this third presentment is "Catholicity;" an explanation of which you, gentlemen, have asked for in these Conferences. Eighteen hundred years ago this Catholic presentment of Christianity went forth into Europe, and, in less than four centuries, captured not only the thinkers but also the masses of Europe. But in the middle ages Romanism arose as a poisoned presentment of Christianity; and afterward, in the Sixteenth Century, Protestantism came on as another poisoned presentment of Christianity. And it is because they are both of them poisoned presentments that the thinking world has virtually rejected both. Very well, what is he cure for all this? Surely Catholics were grossly illogical to say, as Mr. Beecher thinks we say, " Cure one failure by going back to something that had previously failed."

Nay, say we, if Protestantism and Romanism have both failed, let us have the Catholic Christianity once more ; if it be tried for a century or two, it can do again what it has already done; it can regain to Christianity what Protestantism and Romanism between them have lost. A country enjoys the blessings of a constitutional government for six or seven hundred years. It subsequently suffers the evils of a more and more absolute monarchy for a thousand years. Revolt finally supervenes, and it suffers the evils of anarchy for three hundred years; when at last men arise declaring that they have had enough both of tyranny and of anarchy, and demand the constitutional government again. Mr. Beecher calls this going back to Noah's Ark ; he prefers the anarchy.

In the great world to-day Early Church and Catholic Christianity is a still small voice, it is true. But now that Romanism has filled the world with its great strong wind and its fire for 700 years, and Protestantism with its earthquakes for 325 years, possibly the world will listen to something that is not in the wind, and not in the fire, and not in the earthquake.

GENTLEMEN:

In our First Conference we found Catholicity to be a Continent of Certainty, and Protestantism an Ocean of Conjecture. In our Second, we found Catholicity to be a Life and an Organizer and Protestantism a Disorganizer and a Death. In taking up for the last time the subject of Catholicity in its Relationship to Protestantism, let me say that I listen with respect to an objection which I am sure has arisen in your minds since last we met, and which I should have treated at the close of the last Conference, had I not feared exhausting your patience by detaining you too long.

If the Catholic Church is the Body of God Who is still on earth, how is it, you will ask, that It exhibits so many infirmities, not only in the life, but also in the religious opinions of Its members touching points lying outside of the Creed?

All God's great works are composite and intricate. And the answer to this question will advance our conception of the Church; for, as I understand the subject you have assigned to me, it is primarily "Catholicity;" and secondarily "Its Relationship, first, to Protestantism, and secondly to Romanism."

In the first place, then, it is with the Church—it is, that is to say, with the God-man on earth in the centuries, as it was with the God-man in Palestine. In His Divine element He was perfect, indefectable and infinite. But in His human element He was finite; He grew in stature and in wisdom; was often wearied, soiled and hungry; "His visage so marred more than any man that many were astonied at Him;" His poor frame stretched at last and out of joint upon the Cross, bruised and swollen with lashings, thorn-pierced, spear-pierced and dead.

Furthermore, it is with the Church as it is with the Bible. The Bible contains not only a Divine element, but also human elements; the Bible is therefore both infinite and finite, both perfect and imperfect. Parts of It are written in imperfect Greek; Its style is sometimes involved; St. Paul's Epistle to the Laodiceans is gone from It; passages are in It which all agree should be out of It; one-half of the Christian world—more than one-half of the Catholic world even—hold that the Epistle to the Hebrews, St. James'

Epistle, St. Jude's, the Second and Third of St. John, the Second of St. Peter, the verses from the 9th to the 20th in the xvith chapter of St. Mark, the statement concerning the bloody sweat in St. Luke, and other passages here and there, are not fully canonical. The majority of quotations in the New Testament vary from the Old Testament text. In St. Mark, the Magdalen came to the sepulchre at the rising of the sun; but, according to St. John, it was still dark when she came and found the tomb empty. In short, the Bible goes down through the ages bearing the Divine element unharmed within It, but showing at the same time the unsightly bruises and the dark stains of Its human elements with which the Divine is inseparably bound up. The Bible has 925,877 words; and yet while that band of words is organized into the one, perfect, outward body expressive of the infallible message of heaven, each word, in itself considered, is a poor finite word, and each sentence, in itself considered, is liable to imperfections and fallibility.

So also the Church is at the same time infinite and finite, divine and human. Infinite and infallible because It is as a whole the one organic Body of God, expressing perfectly His truth and conveying perfectly His graces; finite, because that Body is made up of human atoms, each of which, individually considered, is fallible and progressive, and of provinces and great Communions, each of which, in itself considered, is liable to imperfections and error. The whole Anglican Church together, therefore, is fallible ; the whole Roman Church is fallible ; the whole Greek Church is fallible. The whole body of bishops is in itself alone a fallible body. For it is to be remembered that God did not promise to be with any part of His Church, however large or small, to preserve that part from error when acting independently of the rest as a definer of new truth. No, He only promised to be with His whole Church and guide It into truth when It acted together as a definer of new truth. However, more of this when we come to Romanism.

Furthermore, with regard to these infirmities in the Church. Man is often compelled to combine many means to produce one end ; but God not seldom brings out one single means to accomplish many different ends. And it is to be remembered that if God is on earth *en rapport* with us, He is here not for a single purpose, but for a two-fold purpose—to meet our two-fold necessities : namely, not only to speak to us all infallibly, but also to cure each of us individually. The Catholic Church is, therefore, under one aspect, the Body of God speaking the perfect truth and imparting grace; but It is also, under another aspect, the human race convalescing. And that theie should be pains during convalescence is not surprising, nay, it is inevitable.

A word or two more touching differences of opinion in the Church on points lying outside of the Creed and of those verities mentioned in the last Conference. Suppose God, having defined through the Church, the essentials of truth, should go on constantly defining new truth on subordinate points as they arise. Should He thus do everything for the individual, should He define all religious truth infallibly, the individual would relapse mentally into leaden inertness in the matter of theology. Christ, therefore, neither does nothing, nor yet does He do all. But while helping the individual where otherwise he would be left helpless, He leaves to each a necessity for action—mental action as well as moral action. This is one of our necessities, and is attended to simultaneously with His other works in the Church. How is it accomplished? Why, outside of the Creed and the verities mentioned in the last Conference, outside, that is to say, of the fundamentals of truth, outside of the essentials of salvation, Christ leaves in the Church a region where mental activity can reverently play, where each can reason on those non-essentials, which are yet not without their importance, where each can investigate, form theories and discuss. The essentials being fixed, no eternal harm follows from temporary differences on other matters.

But at the same time we are all in one Body, we are all in one System, in the centre of which stands, as a sun, the Creed with the essentials of truth. And that sun of truth exerts throughout the system a centralizing force of gravity, which is felt by all the erratic and conflicting theories and reasonings that are within the system, which restrains them from developing and straying to lengths that would be finally disastrous, and which, in the long run, draws them all into sufficiently harmonious revolutions about itself. Thus Catholicity is a system which holds all up to God, holds all up to The Life, holds all up to The Truth. While it is, therefore, the great benign, unifying force, it does not at the same time crush the individuality out of any man. For it is to be borne in mind that if the Body Mystical, the Church, is a creature of God and therefore sacred, so, too, is each separate individual a creature of God and therefore sacred. Neither of these sacred creatures must crush the other. If the Church crushes the individual, or the individual the Church, it is murder. If the Church allows itself to be crushed by the individual, or the individual allows himself to be crushed by the Church, it is suicide. In Romanism the Church crushes the individual. In Protestantism the individual kills the Church. He who perverts from Catholicity to Romanism commits the sin of suicide. He lays himself beneath the wheels of the car of its Juggernaut.

Now, cut off by self-action from this grand, unifying Catholic system, Protestantism is left to fly away from the "Yea" of Christianity into a condition of perpetual and uncontrolled fluctuation and instability touching even the very essentials of truth themselves; and finally to drop off into the utter darkness and nothingness of the "Nay" of Christianity; "while the Son of God, Jesus Christ, Who is preached among you by us," His Priests, "is not yea and nay, but in Him is only yea."

Thus the Church hath the Divine and infallible element of truth and grace bound up into benignant oneness with the fallible and progressive elements of humanity; and, like the Bible, displays sad evidences of its human elements as well as glad evidences of its Divine.

We have only this Conference in which further to treat Catholicity in its relationship with Protestantism. Permit me, then, to present very briefly a third aspect of the two.

Before Jesus Christ came, as the human race had gone into fragments through the fall, so Truth itself was also in fragments. There were glittering shards of Truth in all the ancient false philosophies, in the Kings of China, the Vedas of India, the Zend-Avesta of the Persians, and in every *cultus* of ancient Paganism. Catholicity, coming with Jesus Christ in the centre of time, was the restorer of Truth as well as of man. It was the gathering up and harmonious concentration of all those verities that were dispersed in previous modes of worship. It was the cleanser of them all. It was the supplier of the parts that were lost; and it was the restorer to the world of the rounded sphere of Truth in all its integrity.

But, sixteen hundred years afterward, Protestantism came to smite the rounded truth, and to disperse its fragments broadcast once more. I cannot refrain here from quoting, with slight variations, a striking paragraph of the Count de Maistre's: "Consider," he says, "the Catholic Truth as an assemblage of positive dogmas; the unity of God, the Trinity, the Incarnation, the Real Presence, etc. The sixteenth-century sects denied one and another and another of these dogmas. But those dogmas which they retained are common to Catholicity. So that Catholicity includes all that the sects believe—this is incontestible. The sects, be they what they may, are not *religions*, they are *negations;* that is to say, they are nothing in themselves; for directly they *affirm* anything they are Catholic."

And Mr. Baring-Gould, in one of the most remarkable books of the century, "The Origin and Development of Christianity," admirably illustrates the same truth. "Catholicity," he says, "proclaims the union of the Divine and human natures in Christ. Arianism appeared, and, abandoning more or less completely the first of these two terms, reproduced the second alone. What did Arianism affirm? The humanity of Christ. Catholicity equally affirms this; it believes all that Arianism believed. What did Arianism add to that article of faith? A negation of the first term, i. e., nothing. Catholicity proclaims the co-existence of grace and free-will—that is to say, of divine and human action. Pelagianism started up and left on one side the first of these terms and reproduced the second alone. What did it affirm? The existence of human liberty. Catholicity had affirmed it long before and believed in all that Pelagianism held. What, then, did Pelagianism add to this article of belief? A negation of the first term, *i. e.*, nothing. Catholicity proclaims the double necessity of faith and good works. Luther arose, and omitting the second of these two points, asserted the former only. What did he affirm? The necessity of faith. Catholicity had insisted on this with unchanging voice. What did Luther add? A negation of the second point, *i. e.*, nothing. Finally, Catholicity proclaims the Sacraments, the Eucharistic Sacrifice, the Real Presence, etc. Protestants reject these; in other terms, they substitute for them simple negations, which are nothing. As every heretical or schismatical sect retains this or that verity which suits it, to the exclusion of other truths, and as this process takes place from a thousand different points of view, it is sufficient to add together the articles separately admitted by these communions, mutually antagonistic, to arrive at the sum of all Catholic verities. Also, it is sufficient to strike out the points which each rejects, or to subtract them from the total, to arrive at zero, and thus to show that there is no phase of truth which they do not deny. In the first case they conclude directly for

Catholicity, which is the entirety of which they are the fragments; in the second, they conclude indirectly, by showing that outside of Catholicity is nothing but a process of disintegration of all belief."

But as you stand in presence of the amazing destruction of the sixteenth century, I hear you musing within yourselves and saying, "Surely vast results cannot come from trifling causes; and was there not a reason for Protestantism?"

Certainly, gentlemen, there were mediæval abuses. The Goths and Vandals had swarmed the decks and interior of the Catholic ship as she sailed down time, and brought their unseemly things with them; but how could this be reason for burning and sinking the ship? If God makes the human eye, and inflammation gets into that eye, is that a reason for dashing out the eye itself from the head? There was, indeed, cause for Reformation. But a cause for Reformation is not a cause for destruction. To cleanse a palace by burning it down and tearing up the very stones of its foundation were, surely, the work of folly and of madness. Destruction is a sorry synonym for reformation. The Anglican movement was a Reformation; the Protestant movement was a wide-spread destruction. In England Catholicity was cleansed of its impurities and is saved. On the Continent Catholicity was destroyed and lost. Ah! gentlemen, if philosophy would really account for that torch of the incendiary and knife of the assassin that wrought such havoc in Germany, Switzerland and Scandinavia with the true Catholic dogma, practice and life, it must look deeper than into mediæval abuses. And what is deeper, gentlemen, than the human heart itself? What, since the first resistance of Adam and the fall of man, hath more mysterious chambers? Within it, deep-seated, there is, alas! a basilisk; and that monster is ever ready to rouse himself and resist the principle of submission to Divine authority in matters of Faith. It was not in the Sixteenth Century alone that this basilisk was in the human heart. For, the spirit of resistance to Divine authority has manifested itself more or less in all centuries since the fall. But the Sixteenth Century was exceptional in another respect; for it stood at the close of a long turmoil. It was a vast crisis. Every great war is always followed, like every great tempest, by a ground-swell, which heaves up from the bottom of human nature, and rouses into action, whatsoever is of evil report. And the thirteen hundred long years of continual turmoil and war, in which the ancient polities and civilizations, after centuries of struggle, went down in a vast shipwreck, and out of which modern Europe slowly and painfully emerged, were followed by a recrudescence and exacerbation of that human infirmity and spirit of resistance to God, which appeared, after the fall, in the unhappy Lamech and the defiant Cain.

Indeed, Erasmus said: "I know, as a positive fact, that there never were more luxury and adultery than among the Evangelicals, as they please to call themselves."

George Wizel, in his letters, says: "When I saw the evangelical people reject and ridicule all discipline, all decent living, all that conduces to make men better and truer Christians, and that my sermons, instead of amending hearts, demoralized them, then I began seriously to doubt this doctrine. My doubts gained strength when I saw the debauchery, the hardness, the avarice and pride of the leaders, their endless contradictions, and the discreditable turn the enterprise assumed in other respects."

John Egranus says: "Here are fine results! History is open to demonstrate to us that, during the eight centuries since Germany was Christianized, there has not been in the land a perversity equal tc that which, as every one acknowledges, reigns triumphant now."

Luther himself said that for "one devil of popery expelled, seven worse devils had entered into his evangelicals." And yet in his recklessness he prayed that awful prayer: "O Lord God of heaven, may we be steeped in all kinds of obscenities, in all abominations of sin, rather than fall back into the blindness of Popery; and deliver us from even a spirit of compunction."

Bucer said : "The great bulk of those who joined the reform proposed to themselves the following advantages: freedom from the tyranny of the Pope and the Bishops; that being done, they were all eagerness to give themselves up freely to their caprices and to all their carnal passions. And, indeed, it is to them a most agreeable thing to be able to say, 'We are justified by faith only ; and good works, for which we have no taste, are utterly useless.' Others have favored the preaching of the Gospel solely because it offered them the means of appropriating the goods of the Church. The doctrine of the reign of Jesus Christ has been faithfully announced in a great number of places, I own, but I should be sore puzzled to name a single church where it is practiced, and where Christian discipline is to be found."

Luther describes the state of things. He says: "There is not one of our Evangelicals who is not seven times worse than he was when he was a Romanist—stealing, lying, deceiving, eating and getting drunk, and giving himself up to all kinds of vices."

Indeed, the statistics of crime in one single city show this. There were condemned to death in Nuremberg for incest, highway robbery, murder, infanticide, unnatural crimes, etc., in the fifteenth century, before the Reformation, 41 ; in the sixteenth century, after the Reformation, 190 ; in the seventeenth century, after the Reformation, 272.

Luther wrote to the preacher Riemann: "All the good which we hoped for in this age has vanished as a dream; and in its place a flood of evil is produced which leaves nothing to hope but the dissolution of all things. May the day of God's wrath speedily come to put an end to our miseries and to this infernal disorder." Again he writes : "For the price of the whole world I would not have to begin again. This enterprise brings such agonies with it. Oh, dear Sirs, this is no child's play !"

If such was the case in the sixteenth and seventeenth centuries, what would he have said of the French Revolution of the Protestants in the eighteenth, and of the Commune in the nineteenth centuries?

And so we have, gentlemen, on the Continent of Europe, after the 1,300 years of turmoil, the rousing of the Basilisk, and, as a consequence, not a Reformation, but a Deformation and a hideous destruction. Shall we be stubborn heirs to this fearful legacy? Shall this continue forever?

But, notwithstanding all this, the natural human heart is of itself so much better than the Protestant system, that at last even it has reacted, and has risen, an ally to Catholicity, to restore to some considerable extent common morality.

Permit me next to present to you, in condensed form, a fourth aspect of Catholicity and Protestantism.

As we go up the scale of being, we pass from the simple to the complex; from homogeneous unities to unities each of which contains within itself variety. The simple unity marks a low and imperfect order of existence. The chick is more complex than the egg; the seed, with its radix and two cotyledons, is simpler and lower in the scale of existence than the fully developed tree. If we start from the simple unity of the atom and go up, we come to the more complex unity of the stone. We pass from the stone up to the plant, and find there more diversity still. We pass up to the animal, and we find a still greater variety in the unit; we have matter and instinct. We go up to man only to strike a unit comprehending more variety yet; for we have in him body, instinct, intellect with all its diversity, the moral sense and immortality. And so on up to God, in Whom is the complexity, incomprehensible to us, of three distinct Persons in one undivided Substance. The highest unit, then, is not the unit of simplicity. It is the unit which is differentiated within itself into variety and complexity. Such a unit fills with satisfaction the mind of man and of God. God did not make the solar system one single, enormous globe; nor did He make the earth one smooth sphere of granite. No; while He kept the earth a unit, He developed it into the variations of land and sea, of mysterious mountain and placid lowland, of storm and sunshine, of town and farm, and forest and lake.

Behold, then, in Catholicity the perfect unit, the unit of the highest order. For while Romanism is simple organic unity without diversity, and while Protestantism is diversity without organic unity, Catholicity is organic unity in diversity.

The Oriental type of Catholic man does not object

to the Catholic worship which is in harmony with the Anglican type of man, nor does the Anglican object to the Catholic worship that is in harmony with the Russo-Greek type of man; although each prefers his own for himself. No one is disturbed if national religious habits differ, or if each have his services in his own language.

No two men are alike; and yet God has organized His one visible Church to include all men. It is Itself, then, Catholic and, outside of the fundamentals, tolerant. That there should be schools of thought in Catholicity is unavoidable and not perhaps wrong, so long as those parties do not, in human infirmity, develop the exclusive sect-spirit. In the Catholic Church these two forces, the party-force and the Christ-force, the sundering and the cohesive, are two poles of one power, and perhaps each, in our fallen condition, may be necessary to the healthy existence of the other. As in the solar system there is a centrifugal force to keep the worlds apart and give variety, and a centripetal to bind them, nevertheless, into oneness, so in the domain of the Catholic Church the human spirit of party goes forth into variety, and the Divine power of God goes forth unto unity. Protestantism strikes out the Catholic centripetal force, and flies off and to pieces

Rome strikes out the centrifugal force, and tumbles from the perfect living unit into the unity of simplicity, the unit of the lowest order. In Catholicity, while the rights and prerogatives of the Church are proclaimed and the correlative duties of the individual insisted on, the rights of the individual as a creature of God are not ignored, but respected. While there is hierarchy, there is yet, normally, no tyranny. Over the child is the parent, and over the parent is the Priest, and over the Priest is the Bishop, and over the Bishop is the ecclesiastical authority of the Province, and over that the great Communion or Patriarchate, and over that the whole Catholic Church in space and time. This is the hierarchy. For it is to be remembered that the Church of God is not a democracy, nor a republic; it is the Kingdom of God on earth. The King is Jesus Christ, Who exercises His authority through officers in regular gradation all the way down to the children. This is the hierarchy. And in it each grade, if a father to the grade below it, is itself a child to the grade above. Thus authority is kept from being a school of pride, finding its corrective in humility. For if each grade, except the lowest, has something to command, it has something also above it to obey. This is the hierarchy. "Children, obey your parents, is the law binding on every grade, and it is the mother of order throughout all the ranks. And yet in this hierarchy there is normally no tyranny. For suppose a father should command his child to steal; is the child bound to obey on penalty of breaking the fifth commandment? No. That were tyranny. Even the child has its rights. And the child knows that the Priest is a higher father still, and has forbidden him to steal. And in case of a conflict of commands issuing from the grade above, and the grade above that, the command issuing from the higher grade is to be obeyed, rather than that issuing from the lower, or the fifth commandment is really broken. We must obey the highest parent, all the way up to God. Suppose the Priest should impose on his people something wrong; there is no tyranny in the hierarchy; for the Bishop is the right reverend father to control aright the priest. Suppose the Bishop should set up his private whim as binding upon Priest and people, still there is no tyranny, for the Provincial authority is over the Bishop, and the Bishop is bound to leave free what it leaves free, and to execute its will and law, and not his own private notions. A Bishop once refused to go to the Church of the Advent, Boston. The Priest appealed, and the Provincial authority virtually commanded the Bishop to go. Thus, when the child is in obedience to and in harmony with its parent, and the parents are in obedience to and in harmony with the Priest, and the Priests with the Bishop, and the Bishops with the Provincial authority, and that with the great Catholic Church, which is the Body of and in harmony with Christ, all swing together in obedience to and in harmony with God.

In mediæval times the western part of Catholicity, with all the evils which the Goths and Vandals brought upon it, yet still presented the ancient aspect of variety in unity. Even in later times there were the varieties of the Ultramontane and the Gallican Church. Nations had their different rituals. Why, in Queen Bess's time, the Bishop of Rome offered to accept and acknowledge the Reformed Anglican Church, Ministry, Prayer-book and all, just as She was, if England would only admit his sovereignty over her Queen. But Rome, that never varies, has changed all this. She has brought her pressure upon all to Italianize and Romanize everything; to wipe out all fair varieties, and to reduce everything to a simple uniformity. The Gallican school of thought is crushed. All now everywhere is Jesuit. The Gallican Ritual is abolished; all is Italianized and Romanized. The influence of the great St. Ambrose gave to Milan certain customs, and they held their ground till recently. But Rome will leave no variety; she is slowly wiping what little there is left away. If she clothes an Italian Bishop, who has no diocese, in oriental robes to say Mass, it does not deceive the world that is gazing in attentive neutrality. She will reduce all to the lower order of simple unity in all things. She will brook no variety in unity.

The statement, on the other hand, that Protestantism is utter diversity without organic unity, needs no enlargement or illustration. If there is any apparent unity, it comes from the fact that Protestantism has drifted so far off toward negation that there is little care left in it as to what is believed. And so in my native town, and elsewhere, it has come to pass, at last, that the Unitarian exchanges pulpits with the orthodox Congregationalist. Indeed the belief of the Protestant world has settled down to about this: namely, that there is nothing especially true in Religion; and even if there were, it would not signify.

Permit me now to present to you a fifth aspect of Catholicity in its Relationship to Protestantism. Out of the sacred century I hear the utterance, "In everything ye are enriched by Christ; so that ye come behind in no gift.' Go away, gentlemen, this evening, sit down and seriously ask yourselves, Of what practical use were that marvelous Fountain through Which we may be so enriched that we come behind in no gift, if Its existence is spiritualized away, and Its location is nowhere in particular. Are we, as Christians, to strive to reach Him, after the manner of the modern infidel when he dreamily seeks communion with the God of Nature? A thousand times, no. The Christian's God is a God Incarnate; a God, Who, for our sake, has come forth out of indefiniteness into definiteness. Christianity is not a system that teaches that there is a Church, but no particular Church; and Sacraments but no particular Sacraments; and a Ministry, but no particular Ministry; and Religious Truth, but no particular Religious Truth; and a Lord's Day, but no particular Lord's Day; and a way of Salvation, but no particular way.

The Old Dispensation did not promise to us a mere continuation of God, Omnipresent, Diffusive and Invisible; but it promised something new. It promised Immanu-el; it promised that that God Who is always Omnipresent, should also come and in a special sense be "with us" in the New Dispensation. The perpetual Incarnation of God on Earth, wrought by the marvelous miracles of Font and Altar, is what distinguishes the Christian Dispensation from the Jewish ; it is what distinguishes the Christian's God from the infidel's God of Nature. To suppose, on the other hand, that Christ's Incarnation not only began but also ended with His Body Natural in Palestine—to suppose that that " Stone cut out without hands " was not to " grow and become a great Mountain and fill the whole earth," is to reduce the Holy Sacraments to mere forms, and to remand the world back either to Judaism or to Deism.

It is the Catholic Church, then, that is capable of enriching all men, in everything. As the Church was made by God to include all men, there is no taste or requirement belonging to human nature which It cannot satisfy. There are, indeed, morbid cravings, which arise, not out of the elements that make up human nature, but out of defects in character. These are negative, rather than positive wants. And these the Catholic Church does not respond to. But whatsoever is a positive want, arising out of an element of human nature, that She supplies.

Not so a sect. Some men, for instance, have spiritual and natural requirements which the Quaker sect could not possibly supply. Fancy a Methodist, full of enthusiasm, going into the ice-house of a Friends' Meeting-house. Fancy a man with nature tenderly responsive to the supernatural attempting to find food for his hungers at the empty board of a Unitarian Lecture Hall. Other men have spiritual requirements which the Methodist or the Presbyterian sect could not possibly supply. Men differ; and their differences are so many and so wide apart, that nothing partial, nothing but what is as broad as human nature can meet the wants of each and all. No sect, whatever good it may do to a limited number of persons of similar dispositions, can in the nature of things be co-extensive with man in all space and time. Sects, therefore, always have been and always will be local both in space and time. They always have been and always will be, of comparatively fleeting career,—cut flowers without root, blooming rank for a while, but soon withering away.

Now let us look at man—or rather at men, and see what they are, and what kind of a Church God would, therefore, be likely to provide for them. This will display the relationship between Protestantism and the Catholic Church, and show us where and how it is that any given sect, or all of them together, fail to satisfy the deep and lasting requirements of human nature.

Take for instance any given man. Whoever he is, he is but a very partial representative of our human nature in its fullness. For he may have large imagination and little reason; or large causality and comparison and feeble social qualities; or large social nature and little caution and little reverence; he may have great ingenuity and little memory for names and dates. One man may have love largely developed, and may be reached most easily through that faculty; another can only be reached through his fear; another can be reached through his taste and æsthetical nature; while still another can best be reached only through his reason. Thus no given man is round and full, possessing every human faculty and element, with each in ripe development, and all in perfect harmony with each other. Now each man being thus a partial and imperfect representative of complete human nature, it follows that the wants and hungers of different men, as we find them in life, are widely diverse from each other. They differ according as the elements of our common human nature—reason, ambition, passion, imagination, etc., are combined in different proportions in each. This being the case, what would be the Church that God would provide for men? Surely It would not be fitted merely to meet the wants of any one set of men. Doubtless It would be a Church capable of meeting and supplying all the positive wants of any man. It would be a Catholic Church in the broadest sense of the word. It would be endowed with, and capable of imparting, all supernatural truths possible to the grasp of human nature; even truths which some men can never grasp or hold. It would include, too, all processes to draw men; intellectual, to suit the cold brain; loving, to suit excitable natures; calming, to suit quiet natures; threatenings, for human fears, even though some men may not be timorous; warnings for human caution, even though some men be not cautious; beauty and stateliness to correspond with human taste, even though some men be devoid of the esthetic faculty; and so on. Such is the Church which human endowments and corresponding human needs call for. Such is the Church which God, knowing those human needs, would be likely to organize. Such He has, indeed, provided for the world in The Church Catholic.

But on the other hand, how is it with the sects? How have they subsequently arisen? The Catholic Church is, alas, harassed with differences inside Herself. But why is it that select sets of men separate themselves from the Church Catholic, and maintain their own private "churches?" Let us look at this, and study it a little.

Just as some men are color-blind, and cannot distinguish blue from green, or scarlet from magenta, just as some men cannot tell one piece of music from another, so there are sets of men who are lacking in other respects. Indeed every man is, as I have said, lacking in some respects. And so men fall apart into groups. What then do these several groups do? Take the Congregationalists. Now individual freedom is good; and external authority is good. But each becomes bad if unchecked by the other. Internal freedom, unchecked by external authority, runs out into license. Authority unchecked by freedom, stiffens into tyranny. But, nevertheless, there are some men who have the consummate and irrepressible desire within for the full and free play of all their motions of personal and private will, unchecked by its proper qualifier, viz., the instinct for objective authority of any kind. They are unbalanced. It is hard for them to realize that there can rightly be any external authority bringing itself to bear upon them to check freedom from running into license. Being imperfect and wanting in this respect, these men do not wish to accept God's Church, because It contains something disagreeable to them, namely, an element of authority over all Its members, restraining Its Bishops, Priests and laity from doing, each, just as he pleases. These men, therefore, go forth and form a religious organization with the idea of authority cut out. They set up a Congregational sect; where each parish shall be as independent of every other, and each man in the congregation as independent of every other as possible. Another set of people is lacking in another respect, for instance, in a large and tender sympathy for the Supernatural Objects of Faith, in a sensitiveness to the beings and operations of the unseen world. Now intellect is good and Faith is good. But each needs the other as a check, if intellect is to be saved from stiffening into hardness, coldness and skepticism, and if Faith is to be saved from softening into weakness and superstition. But, unchecked by a due development of the Faith-side of their nature, the intellect of this set of people has sole play. All such supernatural and spiritual facts and beings and operating laws are out of their consciousness. The mention or thought of such is in some sense disagreeable to them. They therefore arrange a Unitarian sect, in which Holy Sacraments, Holy places, Holy (or separate) persons shall be as much excluded as possible ; and where they may enjoy with unalloyed attention the sermon as an intellectual treat. Another set of men have a large sense of the absolute sovereignty and authority of God. But they have this sense to a great degree unchecked and unqualified by its opposite complement, namely, a large sense also of man's free will and responsibility. So, they arrange for themselves, and for others like-minded, a Calvinistic sect. Another set of very excellent people are lacking on the esthetic side of their natures. So, they arrange for themselves a Quaker sect, where not a note of music shall sound, and where the benches and walls shall be unpainted, and where every gay ribbon and bow shall be abolished.

Thus you will perceive that one main peculiarity of sect-ism is, that each sect founds a system and sets it up to suit, not what is *in* human nature, as one of its elements, as a gift of God, but what is *not* in *themselves*. They cut out what the Catholic Church supplies in order that men, who are all partial representatives of human nature, may each be educated, or developed ; in order that that in which each is lacking may be drawn out and enlarged, till we all come to " the measure of the stature of the fulness of Christ," the perfect Man.

Thus each sect is inherently intolerant of just that which it has no taste or talent for, but which it lacks. Each sect is inherently negative and protestant. It cries "Nay-Nay," not "Yea-Yea." You must *not* have music, cries one. You must *not* believe in this, that, or the other doctrine, Sacrament or process, say the several sects all round the circle.

One of the saddest features is, too, that each sect encourages an uneven development of character. Indeed, sectism is the struggle of self-willed man to exclude the disagreeable. Sectism is founded on the satisfaction of " negative cravings"—that is, of morbid hungers that arise out of deficiencies in human character. On the other hand, the Catholic Church was arranged by God to appeal to and satisfy every "positive craving," every hunger and want, that is to say, that arise not out of deficiencies but out of the elements of human nature. The Catholic Church is thus inherently positive, instead of being inherently negative. She is inherently calculated to break down, instead of fostering selfishness and bigotry. For She appeals to and finds Her *raison d'etre* in the fulness of human nature; while the sects find theirs in its defects.

If my spiritual nature and wants and capacity are

partial, what quarrel ought I to have with my brother, if, while I find my wants satisfied, he also finds his different wants satisfied, too, in the ample treasuries of our common home, the Church. Rather should I thank God that my brother's needs are supplied, as well as mine. Surely, I can, and surely I ought, without selfishness, to live at peace side by side with him. What does that man do but erect selfishness within himself, and fan bigotry within himself, what, moreover, does he do but commit the heinous sin of schism, who presumes to take the Catholic Church, which God had provided for us all, and because he and a few of his friends do not, for instance, want anything esthetical and stately in its worship, or because he does not want Priestly absolution, or because he does not want the Sacrament of Confirmation, or because he does not want for himself the rousing storm of a mission, or of a revival, or because he does not want asceticism, or any fasting, or any Saints' Days, or because he does not want to pray for his dear departed wife, child or mother, or because he does not want to cherish a likeness or a religious keepsake of a Saint; if, I say, he presumes to take God's Catholic Church and narrow It to his partial wants and limited horizon by striving to cut out all these things, and thus to deprive his poor brother of them, even though that brother happens to be made a little different from himself in needs, capacities or grasp? No! away with this spirit of selfishness and bigotry and sectarianism, which feels that God's world and God's Church were made for one's own select sect.

God's Catholic Church is like a landscape, that comes behind in no gift to any man. The engineer goes through that landscape ; and he sees and is fed by what his peculiarities crave. He sees, all along, just where he might put a railroad ; just how he will follow the water courses ; just where he is going to get his cuttings for his fillings, and his stone for his culverts, and his wood for his sleepers, and his gravel for his ballast. And the farmer goes through the landscape ; and, lo, the landscape is rich to him, too. He gets out of it its capacity for grains and grapes and grasses ; not but that the farmer would be the more complete man if he also saw with the engineer's eye ; or the engineer, if he saw also with the agriculturist's eye. And the artist goes through it ; and, lo, it presents its exquisite bits of scenery to him. And the geologist goes through it ; and he reads on its upturned leaves the history of the past. The spirit of Catholicity would cry, "Let it alone: let us each get all out of the landscape that ever we can." But the spirit of sect would go there and would strip it of its deep and infinite supplies to meet the wants of diverse men, leaving only what would satisfy its own peculiar self.

Just because each and every man is a partial and not a complete representative of human nature, just because each man is wanting in some elements of character, so do they all need a Whole Church capable of educating all the elements of character. But sectarianism says, on the other hand, because men are fragmentary, so must we break up that Church into little pieces—so that one piece shall have and teach God The Father and the four Gospels alone, without the Atonement or God The Son, or much else, and another piece shall teach the Trinity and the Atonement without the Sacramental System, or much else; and another piece shall teach free will without God's sovereignty; and another, God's sovereignty without free will; and another, faith without works; and another, works without faith; and another, dipping in Baptism without pouring; and another, pouring without dipping; (and so on through the whole diapason of doctrines and practice;) and then let us draw as many men as we can out of the great

Cathedral with its many windows alow and aloft, letting in the light from all around, nave, clere-story, transepts, lady-chapel, lantern, choir, east end, and west end, and shut them up in our little room with its one or two windows letting in light at one side, one end or one corner only.

God has made His Catholic Church, and endowed It with every gift, not only that all may find in It what they severally crave, but that each also may be schooled in what he may be wanting.

But the sectarian cries to all the world, out of his deficiencies and out of the antipathies which those defects rear within him, "Come to our sect; you do not like Confirmation; neither did we; that is our 'nay;' we have founded a sect on that 'nay;' come to us; you will not find any Confirmation with us:" or, "Come to our sect, you hate enthusiasms in religion; so do we; that is our 'nay;' we have founded a sect accordingly; come to us, you will not find any revivals among us:" or, "There is a deal of music in the world, indeed, but you do not like music, you think it is wicked; so do we; music is our 'nay;' we have founded a sect on our lacks, where we have no music, but sit still for the Spirit to move us:" or "Come to our sect; you hate these Religious; so do we; we have founded a sect on our and your deficiencies and dislikes ; you will not find any monks and nuns with us:" or " You do not like anything stately and beautiful in worship; neither did we; we have founded a sect on our deficiencies in taste ; you will not find any boy-choirs or processions or ritual with us." And so on to the end of the list of ' Nays.'

But come, saith God, come, says Catholicity with Her " Yeas," come to the Church. Do you want freedom ? You will find freedom here. Do you want authority? You will find it here. Do you want the contemplative and praying life ? You will find it here. Do you want the active, secular life ? You will find it here. And so through all the wants that arise, not out of the defects, but out of the endowments of human nature.

If any part of the Catholic Church through the lapse of the centuries grows untrue to Her functions, and therefore untrue to man to whom She is sent, that part must expect one of two things ; either a struggle and a turmoil within Herself till She takes up again and uses the weapons against the world which have been allowed to lie idle and to rust in her armories ; or if this does not take place, She must expect sects to spring up around Her as Her punishment. For human nature will have neither tyranny nor license, skepticism nor superstition, baldness nor mere empty formalism.

But there is another divine economy in the Catholic Church, which lifts Her immeasurably above any sect. If all men were made exactly alike in character, development and grasp, all would be equally receptive, and the Church would be able to impart a fixed amount of Her exhaustless gifts to each. But first, all men start away in life, ignorant and devoid of even a single one of the gifts and truths which the Church bestows. Then, secondly, men develop afterwards into differences of grasp ; their circumstances are such, too, that their opportunities and time for acquiring systematic, moral and ascetic theology, and for attaining spiritual growth, differ. No man, indeed, however aged and able, is ever in such position that he may not learn yet more than he already knows, that he may not attain to higher grades of spirituality, that he may not look deeper into truths he has already received, or the better understand the relationship which these profound truths bear to each other. On the other hand, the Catholic Church contains all spiritual, theological, moral and ascetic truth, each in its entirety. These are all, not actually, but potentially, made over to each member of the Church, that all the members may severally come into actual possession of as much as ever each one can. Each one, whether he is a child learning his catechism, or a youth in the Bible class, or a young man, a middle-aged or an old man, should thank God for all he knows or has assimilated to himself; but his true attitude is not to deny what, either through his want of grasp, or want of years, or want of opportunity and time, or want of complete development as a representative of human nature, he does not yet receive. He should enjoy his actual possessions, and not be resistant to, or protestant against, those potential possessions which are his nevertheless, which have been made over to him by the Church, as though they were false because he has not happened to hear of them before, or been able to grasp or profit by them.

Now if I had a museum, an academy containing facilities for learning all of art, and of fine art, of manufacture, and geology, and botany, and languages, and every science, and, indeed, all knowledge, and if I put into it a hundred thousand men of different tastes and capacities, as into a school, I have enriched them, each and all; I have held back from no one, anything. There would, therefore, be no possibility, either for the mind of any one of them to fail of its own proper food, or for any mind among them all to have a stunted growth.

Now the Catholic Church of God is analogous to such a complete school. No sect is a universal school. What is the difference, then, between a man in the Church and a man in a sect? In a sect he has grasp of partial truth. But no one in the Church has complete grasp of the whole truth either. So there is no difference here. Nevertheless, the Catholic Churchman has an immense advantage over the other. For even if he also has not actual grasp of the whole round of Catholic truths, and even if he does use some only of the whole circle of Catholic appliances tending to a complete spiritual and moral growth and development, he is at any rate in the Church where all the rest of the truths and appliances are; he is not cut off from them; they are all potentially his, and may happily, sooner or later, one after another, become actually his, to his great enrichment and advantage. God does not expect the child to be as far advanced in learning or growth as the youth, or the youth as the adult, or the young man as the old man, or those with partial opportunities for attaining all that is possible to be attained as those with full. But, on the other hand, take this same person out of God's Catholic Church and put him in a sect, which simply presents doctrines and practices with which the tide of his partial development and defective character is merely on a level, and behold, he is absolutely cut off from all the rest of the circle of truth, and from all the rest of the round of appliances. Nay, worse, he is not only cut off from them, but he is encouraged in prohibiting them to himself. What hope is there, then, except that such a man must have a narrow, bigoted, stunted religious development and life.

Some of you, gentlemen, are already Catholic Churchmen.. Have you carried these thoughts, of which I am to-night the mouth-piece, out to their legitimate conclusions in your hearts? I am here it is true for a course of conferences, and not of sermons. I am here to speak to your heads and not to your hearts. But suffer me, if, for a moment, I transgress the bounds of my present mission, and do not forget that I am a Priest speaking to men who have hearts as well as heads. Let me remind you, then, that in God's great Church the Catholic has no quarrel with the Low Churchman. The *truths* which the Low Churchman holds, he holds in common with us. God bless him as he carries the great truth of the Atonement, the Cross of our Blessed Saviour, without which we are all lost, on and out into a sinful world. God bless him, as, full of zeal and of the love of souls, he gathers earnest men around him in his lecture room, that he may exhort them and that they may exhort each other and pray with each other. We hold everything which he holds; but we hold a great deal more besides of the great round of Catholic truth. We can join him in his prayer meeting; but let us have no quarrel with him if, after the meeting is over, he will not go with us, besides, to the Altar and fall down in adoration before our Lord Christ and God. The difficulty comes in where he, instead of being passive as to the additional and not incompatible truths, actually denies them for us as well as for himself, and, in a spirit of sectism, has a fierce quarrel with us for accepting from the Church and believing a little more than he does.

Now, my Catholic friends, let us beware on our side of that self same spirit of sectism, which would prompt us to drive him out of the Church because he holds only a part and not what we claim to be full truth as set forth in the formularies of the Church. For if, like bigoted sectarians, we drive him out where could he go except into something where he would be actually cut off from learning those blessed truths?

But, besides, there is another reason why we have, on our side, no quarrel either with our Low Church or with our old fashioned High Church brethren; but rejoice rather that they are all in the Church, and hope that one and all will stay. And that is, because, even if we are fully conscious that they have not yet received all the truth which the Church has to impart to them in Her Prayer Book, we ourselves, even though we receive a little more than they, are by no means graduates. For we all are learners, as I have said, and always will be, in Her vast school of infinite truth. And we shall never, any of us, learn the whole, till we get into that Higher School where we shall see the Lord face to face in Beatific Vision. The fact is, we are simply all of us, Low, High and Catholic, standing at different positions on an inclined plane of grasp, opportunity and receptiveness; while Christ, through the Church, stands ready to enrich us all in everything, so that we come behind in no gift.

Let us have, I say, no quarrel whatever with them Let us pray God that they may cease their quarrel with us; and that we may all love each other, and bear with each other, and pray for each other, and work with each other, and think no evil of each other; knowing that we shall all do well, if we only continue sitting in humility and teachableness around the knee of our great, kind, patient Mother the Church Catholic; and realizing more fully, the more we learn, how dangerous a little learning is; how full it is apt to be of the spirit of arrogance, bitterness and hardness; for down to a certain point the less a man knows, alas, the more he thinks he knows.

GENTLEMEN:—You have assigned to me three Conferences on Catholicity and Protestantism. In bidding farewell to this first half of our subject, let us see to what we trace back Catholicity, and to what we trace back Protestantism. We follow Catholicity back, with its stately Rituals and comforting dogmas, to the sixteenth century; back through the middle ages to the ages of the Six Great Councils; back to St. Ignatius, Bishop of Antioch, to St. Polycarp, Bishop of Smyrna, to St. Clement, Bishop of Rome, whose name St. Paul says is written on the Book of Life, to St. Timothy, Archbishop of Ephesus, and St. Titus, of Crete, to Sts. Andrew, John and James, and up to Him who said, "Blessed are the pure in heart, for they shall see God; blessed are the meek, for they shall inherit the earth; blessed are they which do hunger and thirst after righteousness, for they shall be filled; blessed are the merciful, for they shall obtain mercy." We follow it up to Him who was much in worship, much in holy meditation, much in prayer.

We follow Protestantism back to the sixteenth century and up to Martin Luther, on the other hand, who, writing of holy meditation and prayer, said: "When the monks, sitting in their cells, meditated on God and His works, when, inflamed with the most ardent devotion, they bowed the knee, prayed and contemplated heavenly things with so much delight that they shed tears; here was no thought of women nor of any other creature, but only of the Creator and His marvelous works. And yet this thing, most spiritual in the judgment of reason, is, according to Paul, a work of the flesh. Wherefore all such is religious idolatry; and the more holy and spiritual it is in appearance, the more pernicious and pestilential it is." I do not know, I am sure, why Scientific Meditation has so become a lost art in Protestant lands that we have to teach the art all over again; I do not know why worship has so died away that meeting-houses are shut up from Sunday night to the subsequent Sunday morning. I do not know why it should be that when in Mecklenburg, an inquiry was made into the state of the Established Lutheran Church in 1854, " it was ascertained that, in the three head churches of the Principality, there had been no divine service two hundred and twenty-eight times, because there had been no congregation." I do not know how it is that the Hartford (Conn.) *Courant* should have informed the world ten years ago thus: " The Congregational ministers of Connecticut have thoroughly convassed their parishes to ascertain the actual religious condition of the State. The result was unexpected. In one hundred towns at least one-third of the families are not in the habit of going to church. Irreligion was found to increase in proportion to the distance from the centre of towns. It prevails more in sparsely-settled farming districts than in the manufacturing villages. The Committee on Home Evangelization say in their published report: 'The returns give the impression that the Roman Catholic population do not often sink to so low a grade of heathenism as the irreligious native-born population. They do not entirely abandon some thought of God, and some respect for their religious observances. *Uniformly the districts most utterly given over to desolation* are districts occupied by a population purely native-American. A similar state of things is reported to exist in some parts of Massachusetts.'" I do not know why prayer hath so died away. I only know what the Solifidian, Luther, said.

We trace Protestantism back to Luther, who said, again: "Thou seest how rich is the Christian; even if he will, he *cannot* destroy his salvation by any sins how grievous soever, unless he refuse to believe." Who said again: "Be thou a sinner and sin boldly, but still more boldly believe and rejoice in Christ. From Him sin shall not separate us; no, though a thousand times in every day we should commit fornication or murder." Who said again; "If in faith an adultery were committed, it were no sin." To Martin Luther, who said: "The Gospel does not bid us *do* anything, or bid us leave anything *undone;* it exacts *nothing* of us; quite the contrary. In place of saying, 'Do this, do that,' it simply requires us to spread out our lap and accept, saying, 'Hold! see what God has done for you, and given His own Son to be incarnate for you: accept the gift, *believe*, and you are saved.'" And again: "You owe nothing to God, nothing, except to believe and confess Him. In everything else He leaves you perfect liberty to do exactly what you like, without any peril for your conscience; even—for

He is quite indifferent to it—you may abandon your wife, or desert your husband, or not keep any engagement you have contracted, for what concern is it to God whether you do these things or not?' To Luther, who wrote again to one suffering from remorse on account of his sins: "Drink, play, laugh and do some sin even as an act of defiance and contempt to the devil. Therefore, if the devil says to you, 'Don't drink so,' do you reply to him, 'Aye, I will drink all the more copiously in the name of Christ.' Thus do just contrary to that which Satan (*i. e., conscience*) prompts. One can drive these Satanic thoughts away by introducing other thoughts, such as that of a pretty girl, avarice, drunkenness, or by giving way to violent passion: *such is my advice."*

We trace Protestantism back to Melancthon, who said : "Whatever thou doest, whether thou eatest, drinkest, workest with thy hand, I may add shouldst thou even sin therewith, *look not to thy works ;* weigh the promise of God." Who said again, " God ought not to displease you when He damns the innocent. All things take place by the eternal and invariable will of God, Who blasts and shatters in pieces the freedom of the will. God creates in us the *evil* in like manner as the good. The high perfection of faith is to believe that God is just, notwithstanding that by His will He renders us necessarily damnable." And again: "We cannot advise that the license of marrying more wives than one be *publicly* introduced. There is nothing unusual in princes keeping concubines; and although the lower orders may not perceive the excuses of the thing, the more intelligent know how to make allowance."

We trace Protestantism back to Calvin, who said that God instigates man to the commission of what is evil, and that man's fall into crime is ordained by the providence of God. To Zwingli, who asserted that God "is the author, mover and impeller to sin," and that He uses the instrumentality of man to produce injustice; " He it is who moves the robber to murder the innocent." We trace Protestantism back to Beza, who said: "The Almighty creates a portion of men to be His instruments, with the intent of carrying out *His evil designs* through them."*

But, O Jesus, Thou didst teach thy Catholic Church that "God is love!"

Mr. Beecher, in his remarkable sermons of last

* I am indebted for many of these extracts from the Reformers to Mr. Baring-Gould, who, in his "Origin and Development" and "Luther and Justification," gives the references.

Sunday, in admitting, even more fully than one had charged, the wide-spread prevalence of atheism, pantheism and infidelity generally in Protestant lands, and even in Protestant churches themselves, says: "No matter; Christianity, nevertheless, will not die." Of course not; for Catholicity still stands with its rounded sphere of truth, and the Gates of Hell will not prevail against It. And even Protestantism, in dashing the sphere to flinders, holds for a while shattered shards of it. The sun of Catholicity, sending its gravitating force even beyond its own system and into the outer spaces, has had, and will have a restraining power. It is the system of Protestantism that has been attacked in these lectures, not any man—not any man, living or dead; not even the shockingly sinful Zwingli, nor the unhappy, conscience-tormented Luther. Systems may be hateful, but all men are dear; and false systems are hateful because all men are dear.

If Protestantism be not a failure, if the Anglican Church as a double witness against Protestantism and Rome be not right, in God's name let it be known. For we speak in sorrow, not in anger, to friends and respected brothers, all of whom love Jesus Christ and His Name as much as we do; and we seek not victory, but truth.

FOURTH CONFERENCE.

FUNCTION OF REASON IN RELIGION. DIFFERENCE BETWEEN THE CATHOLIC AND THE ROMAN IDEA OF THE UNITY OF THE CHURCH.

GENTLEMEN,

God has given to each of us the gift of reason; and we have no right either to destroy or to misuse a gift of His. The proper exercise of reason is, therefore, a responsibility from which no human being can escape. The function of reason is unlimited in the natural realm, except by the theological virtue of Faith and by the Fifth Gift of the Holy Ghost, namely, the Gift of Knowledge. Reason hath its function in the supernatural realm also. For if God is on earth in a speaking Body, or Catholic Church, we must, first of all, be convinced of that fact. Reason, therefore, is the prelude of faith. Being convinced, we afterwards accept, without arguing, what God through His Catholic Body states to be the Truth.

But there is a preliminary difficulty. What is this Catholic Body? Two different theories concerning this point present their claims to us. Fortunately there are only two. Rome claims that she alone is this Catholic Church. The Anglican Communion claims that the Catholic Church includes all the Communions that have the Apostolic and Catholic Ministry, Faith and Sacraments. What are we to do then in presence of these two differing theories, the inclusive and the exclusive? Clearly we cannot escape the responsibility of still further exercising our private judgment, and of deciding, each for himself, which of these two claims is right.

But before we go on, let us see what it is we have already settled in our minds. You will remember that in our First Conference the hand of logic led us into a certain conclusion. That conclusion was, that Almighty God, having broken through the dome of Nature and come in among us to save us from drowning in mere guess-work touching Supernatural law and fact here and hereafter, remained *en rapport* with us in a continuous organic Body of human matter, called the Visible Body Mystical of Christ, or Holy, Catholic and Apostolic Church. This, you will remember, was the answer to the Second Great Question with which we were brought face to face in our search for the truth.

When we thus speak of an organic body we mean

a body which has correlated parts; *i. e.* differing members whose functions are reciprocal, and whose inter-action is orderly. Now, incidentally, we may remark, that historic fact bears out the logical conclusion at which we have arrived. For nothing is more certain than that the Christian Body, that stood on earth eighteen hundred years ago, was an organic and visible Body. As we read the sacred Epistles we find them addressed to the saints at Ephesus, at Corinth, at Colosse. We find them containing instructions and rules for those saints. It appears, then, that some parts of this organic Body were rulers and others were the ruled. We also see, early in the Gospels, allusions made to two of its Sacraments; and afterwards, in the Gospels, the Acts and the Epistles, we find that these two, with a third and others, are regularly arranged as a part of the organic Body, and commanded to be used. Christ saith to the Apostles, " All power is given unto Me both in Heaven and Earth ; " " Go ye, therefore, Baptise all nations ; " " teach them ; " " Do, (*i. e.* offer) This as a Memorial of Me ; " " Whosoever sins ye remit they are remitted unto them." We read, moreover, as follows, viz., " Ordain elders in every city ; " " The husband is the head of the wife, as Christ is the head of the Church.

This is a great Sacrament, but I speak concerning Christ and the Church;" "Then laid St. Paul his hands upon them, and the Holy Ghost came on them;" "Let them pray over him, anointing him with oil in the name of the Lord."

Thus we see an organic Body created, with Sacraments, with members whose function it was to rule, to instruct, and to administer those Sacraments; and with members whose function it was to be the recipients of those teachings, of that discipline and of those Sacraments. Nothing is more certain than that, in the organization of that Christian Body, in the appointing and arranging of its correlative parts, and in the commission of its rulers, God, *i. e.* Christ, worked directly. On Whitsunday God the Holy Ghost descended upon this Body or Church to fill It with Himself, and to make It, as an organic Body, a living and life-giving appliance unto the world. Later on, the Holy Ghost commands the rulers of the Body to commit the powers they had received to others, faithful men; that those powers and functions might continue in the Body, and not cease through the death of their original possessors. Thus nothing is more certain than that, as an historical fact, **God Himself organized a visible Church on earth.**

This divinely organized Church had, furthermore, a two-fold function to perform : first, a pastoral function; to build up, namely, Its own members in the truth and in godliness of life; and, secondly, a missionary function; to spread, namely, into all the world, and to gather into Its bosom and into oneness with Itself all peoples. And the promise is given to this Divine Catholic organism, that It should not die, that Its Soul should not depart from It, " Lo, I am with you always even unto the end of the world."

Nothing is more certain than that this entire Organic Body, with the light with which It was endowed, with Its truth-dispensing officers and grace-dispensing Sacraments, was arranged on earth by a loving God for the benefit of an ignorant and sinful race. Nothing is more certain than that, prior to its existence, men were in darkness touching some of the most important and saving truths and ways of eternal life ; and that light as to these matters did spread forth among men from this Organic Body as a centre, and from It alone, until Polytheism and its rites fell all over Europe, and Olympus was depopulated. Hence, as this Body was to be a Divine Teacher and Dispenser of grace, an Administrator of Christ and of His truths and of His gifts unto men, it is evident that It could not have been a mere ephemeral creation. God did not organize It on earth for some men or for a few generations only; but for all men in all time; "Go ye: baptise all nations." Indeed Christ promised to be with It till the end. *A priori*, It possessed, as an organic Body, a continuous and sacred life; a continuous life and succession in Its Ministry, in Its Sacraments, in Its Faith, and in Its Traditions. It must therefore, as an organic undying Body, with Its rulers and teachers, Its ordinances, rites, worship and light-giving powers, have passed on through the centuries, and It must be in existence to-day.

To kill It, is the essential act of murder, of which all other murders are mere types; for, to kill It, is no less than the murder of God on earth, the repetition of the tragedy on Calvary. To rob It of Its powers, is the essential theft, of which all other thefts are types. To set up a sect as a rival to It, that that sect may bear children unto Christ, is the essential whoredom and adultery, of which all other adulteries are but types. And when the essential adultery has been committed by a great people, it is comparatively easy for them to look less sternly than they should on all other adulteries, and to demand of their State Legislatures laws of easy divorce. Wilfully to misrepresent and slander It, is the essential false-witness, of which all other lying is a type. For, the four laws of the Second Table, in which man's duty to man is summed up, Thou shalt not hurt thy neighbor in his person, in his property, in his good name, or in his chastity, have their origin philosophically and theologically not in the arbitrary will of God, or in the well-being of man, but in the archetypal structure and well-being of God Himself. All injury to man is sin, because it is a type of an awful and corresponding outrage upon God. Protestantism therefore is a sin, because it is a fearful attack on the well-being of God on earth.

But to return; if this Catholic Church, organized by God 1800 years ago, is in existence to day, as I am one of those human beings, sinful and ignorant by nature, for whom Christ came and for whom He organized His Church, as I need light and Sacraments and guidance from divinely appointed superiors as much as any one ever did in ancient Palestine, or Corinth, or Ephesus, or Rome, or Antioch, I may not therefore, pick and choose my ecclesiastical connections to-day among societies that any men have since organized. As God Himself organized a Church for me 1800 years ago, and promised to be with It till the end of time, I am left with no choice whatever in the matter. If He had organized no Church Which was to exist continuously, and with Which *He* was to be till the end of the world, but had left men to organize, sixteen hundred years afterwards, as many different "churches" as they chose, I then might select from among them any one that pleased my fallibility; or I might even set up a new one for myself; for I would have as much right to organize a new church as any one else. But who am I? I am not a Creator. I cannot make either a new Church, or a new Sacrament, any more than I can create a new particle of matter.

But, I hear you say, what are we to do in case God's Catholic Church should, on account of the human infirmity that is in It, so decline as to need a reformation in some respects? Ought we not to abandon Its Ministry and Sacraments, and go out from It, as did Luther? But this were to give up faith in God. First, never should we cut ourselves off from the life-giving and life-sustaining Sacraments Such infirmities in the Church as you speak of cannot poison the grace that God gives through His Sacraments, any more than impurities in the air can alter the sweet tones of a lute as they pass to my ear; for the Church is perfect as well as imperfect. And, secondly, if the Church ever needs a reformation, to abandon It were to fly from our post as one of Its forces of cure, and to forget Christ's promise to be with It. Surely that promise is sanction that It will throw off Its disease by the internal action of Him, Who is within It as Its strong health-giving constitution.

Reformation? Why this world is the realm of an imperfect state of things at the best. Perfection in all things is not to be hoped for even in the Church. How then was such inevitable imperfection and liability to err and to need reform to be managed? God came and organized it all into His Divine Catholic Church. I am sure He knew best how to deal with and cure the diseases of His Church, and that I have no need to kill His Church on account of Its falling ill. If I feel that I cannot do very much towards curing Its diseases, I can at least do something; I can do more within It than I can if I were without Its pale. And, at any rate, I must not forget that God remains in His Church as Its principle of recovery. Surely I should stay with Him, and coöperate with Him. If It does not in every century keep on the exact mathematical straight line of perfection in all things, I am sure that any other plan than God's for dealing with the imperfection would, in the long run, only leave matters infinitely worse off for time and eternity. A fool is he who thinks he can mend or do better than God's work. I stand aghast before the result that would have happened, had it been Protestantism instead of Catholicity that the Goths and Vandals overwhelmed and threw into the trough of the sea. Europe would have foundered and gone down.

Since God, then, has organized a Church on earth for the world, I have, I say, no liberty whatever in the matter; I must belong to that Church. If that Church has Sacraments I must be baptized with Its Baptism and must feed at Its Altars, and at no others. I cannot countenance any others, even by my presence. For I should be countenancing by my presence and connivance the essential robbery, the essential murder, the essential slander and the essential adultery themselves. If that Catholic Church has rulers and teachers to guide its members and to dispense the Faith, of which It was made the divine receptacle, I must receive that Faith from them. With filial trust I must come to that Church, strive to do my duty according to Its directions, and with perfect assurance, leave all the rest to God. As to Its Faith, It cannot fail; but if It fall ill in mere doctrine or manners, I must stand by It and do my part towards effecting Its cure.

Having reached this point, namely, Catholicity, you will remember that we paused, before proceeding to any subsequent questions, to examine the general characteristics of the Catholicity into which we thus found ourselves forced.

In our second Conference we found that this Catholicity was a Life and an Organizer; while Protestantism was a Disorganizer and a Death. We found, secondly, that the Omniscient God in His Body on Earth utters through It to us and to the world the Nicene Creed as the Infallible Truth, and that He sets forth certain other fundamentals of truth. Now faith, which comes in after all this exercise of our reason and private judgment, is not an acquiescence in our own opinions, but an humble reception of what is thus spoken by God. We believe the Creed, that is to say, not because we think what is said in it is reasonable; not because it suits our fancy; not because we have studied its truths out for ourselves; but only because God Himself speaks it daily to mankind. But having accepted, without arguing, this infallible statement of supernatural truth and the way of salvation, we are surely permitted afterwards to examine and admire the Gift we have received. Nay it were an indignity both to the Gift and to the Giver if we did not examine it with our grace-enlightened reason. Here, then, is another function of reason in the Church. We, therefore, then reverently analyzed the Creed; and glanced at the havoc which Protestantism had wrought in it by tearing it into separate pieces.

In the following Conference, we found, thirdly, that the Catholic Church was both Divine and human; and displayed, therefore, not only perfections but imperfections; that outside the Creed there was a region in the Church where mental action was allowed to play; that, owing to certain human imperfections, a reformation of the Western part of the Church became necessary in the sixteenth century; that such Reformation took place in England; but that on the Continent it went beyond all bounds, and assumed, instead, the form of a Destruction of Catholicity. We found that medieval abuses were, as causes, inadequate to account for that fell and mad destruction. And we traced the real cause of Protestantism to that basilisk in the fallen human heart, which is ever ready to resist the principle of submission to Divine Authority in matters of faith, and which thirteen hundred years of war and turmoil at last availed to rouse into terrible action.

We found, fourthly, that while fragments of truth were dispersed among the religions and philosophies of the ancient world, Catholicity came in the fulness of time, gathered these fragments together, and completed the rounded sphere of truth for the world; but that, sixteen hundred years subsequently, Protestantism smote that sphere of truth into fragments again, to lose them in infidelity.

We found, fifthly, that while Romanism was organic unity without diversity, and Protestantism was diversity without organic unity, Catholicity was the highest form of unity, namely, organic unity in variety.

And we closed by glancing at the frightful solifidianism of Luther and his fellow-heretics, and the consequent wreck of even common morality in Protestant lands during the sixteenth and seventeenth centuries.

All this time we have been resting back, I repeat, at the answer to our Second Great Question, and examining the general characteristics of the Catholicity into which we had been led. We have now reached a time when we must look up and go on. But, in the Catholic pathway before us, the road divides again, and we are face to face with our Third and last Great Question.

For as I move forward to unite myself with the Catholic Body, I am suddenly confronted with two Bodies, each visible, each claiming to be Catholic, each claiming to have had a continuous organic life from the Apostles, each claiming the continuous Catholic Ministry, Faith and Sacraments. They are, indeed, alike in some respects; they differ in others. What am I to do? There is nothing for me to do but to pause before them, listen to their claims and decide between them.

In what do they agree? In accepting the Six Great General Councils of the first seven hundred and eighty years of the life of Catholicity; in holding the Nicene Creed; in having Bishops, Priests and Deacons; in the necessity of the Apostolical Succession; in the Sacraments and Sacramental System; in Baptismal Regeneration, the Eucharistic Sacrifice and the Real Presence; in prayers for the dead; and in a Ritual form of worship. Concerning these points, then, we have nothing to do now. I shall hereafter, merely however for brevity's sake, include all this, about which there is no question, under the name of The Nicene Creed.

But over and above these, Roman Catholicism has erected certain additional dogmas, which it declares to be necessary to salvation. These, Anglican Catholicity declares to be either false, or not necessary to salvation.

The first of these points of difference which I shall take up is this, namely; the two bodies, Roman and Anglican, differ as to what constitutes the unity of the Church. Both hold that the Church is one; but Rome sets up the exclusive theory; She claims that She alone is that Catholic church; in other words that the church is one like a single individual; and that whosoever is not in agreement and communion with the Bishop of Rome is not in the Catholic Church at all. Formerly She did not claim this. To-day, since the late Vatican decree, She claims it. Anglican Catholicity, on the other hand, declares this to be a novel and modern idea, an alteration of the ancient idea. Anglican Catholicity holds up the inclusive theory. Its conception of the Catholic Church includes every Communion which, accepting the Nicene Creed and the Six General Councils, possesses also an Apostolic Ministry, and therefore the Sacraments, and therefore the Catholic Sacramental life; in other words that the visible Catholic Church is one like a family, rather than one like a single individual and that the Bishop of Rome, by excommunicating and anathematizing from time to time all who do not agree with him in every additional dogma, which Rome from time to time has defined, has been placing himself out of communion with more and more of the Catholic Church, and has brought trouble and fearful discord into the Catholic Body; that Satan, desiring to have him, is indeed "sifting him like wheat;" that he is indeed denying the Lord thrice, with anathemas, and curses; that he is indeed impetuous and full of zeal, full of the things of this world, calling down upon himself the Lord's solemn prophecy, "Get thee behind me, Satan; thou art an offence unto me; for thou savourest not the things that be of God, but those that be of men;" that he has altered the old Apostolic theory of the unity of the Church; and that by the side of that old theory, the Catholic Church, as defined by Rome, shrinks into something like a mere sect and the prolific mother of sects.

Catholic Christendom, then, presents itself in two vast and separate divisions; namely, first, Catholics not in communion with the see of Rome, and, secondly, Catholics in communion with that see. The former division comprises within itself the Greek Catholics, the Armenian and Georgian Churches, the Anglican Catholics and the Alt-Catholics—in all, something over one hundred millions of souls. The latter division comprises the Roman Catholics alone; in all, about a hundred and seventy millions of souls. So that while Protestants number seventy millions, the Catholics number two hundred and seventy millions. The former division of Catholics, comprising the Greeks and the Anglicans with others, we may designate under the generic title of "Catholics" or "Old-Catholics;" the latter division under the generic title of "New-Catholics," or Roman Catholics. The Old Catholic Communions agree in asserting the paramount importance of maintaining the old Apostolic constitution which the Catholic Church presented in the first five centuries, and in maintaining that Roman Catholicism is one of the most modern of Religions.

Let us, then, to this question of what it is that makes the unity of the Catholic Church. Rome claims that unless a person agrees with the views in addition to the Nicene Creed, which have been announced by the Pope in successive centuries subsequent to the Eighth, he is out of the Catholic Church and not a Catholic at all. Döllinger, Reinkens and thousands of others, Alt-Catholics, could not give intellectual assent to the dogma of the Pope's infallibility, and were, therefore, excommunicated from itself by the Roman part of the Church. But the mistake of Rome is, that she thus rests the unity of the Church on something which flows from man; namely the harmony of men's wills and the consenting of their minds with the will and mind of the Pope; and that she no longer rests the unity on something that flows from God. No: a mere consenting together of minds cannot create a supernatural and divine organic unity. For however two men may agree together in certain conclusions and become *friends*, this cannot create them *brothers* and of one flesh. The unity of the Church is something that flows not from man or anything man can do, but it is a gift from God. As God alone could make the natural race of man organically one in Adam, so He alone can make the supernatural Church organically one in Christ. Its organic unity is derived from the New Adam, Christ, in a certain way. We are grafted, namely, into Christ by God in Baptism, and this unity is then continued and completed by Christ's Body and Blood in the Eucharist, Which not only incorporate Him into us, and us into Him, but us into each other as a one Communion—a one Body. We are one, not because we agree in intellectual or historical conclusions; but because we are all thus made one with Christ He it is, that is the foundation and cause of our unity. This organic unity descends from the Head to the Body, uniting the Body to the Head and the parts of the Body to each other. Thus our true supernatural union *with one another* is not a mere agreement of minds, but an organic union made by God, as He unites us all to the one Christ and to each other by the Catholic life-giving and curing Sacraments.

If mere discord of men's minds could of itself break this organic Churchly unity, then a mere concord of men's wills and minds could of itself create such a unity. But this would make man able to create a Church, to create organic unity, by something going out from himself. And, therefore, a mere human society, a temperance society, a political party, agglomerating together, could become of itself as organically one supernaturally, as the race is organically one naturally. Why, this Roman Catholic theory of unity is the very theory of Protestantism itself; and therefore the Pope is the greatest and most magnificent Protestant of them all. And we are justified in saying that the Catholic Church, as defined by Rome, shrinks into something like a mere sect.

No, the Catholic Church is one like a family, not

one like a single individual. The three or four Sisters may unhappily fall out among themselves; they may not speak to each other; they may not eat at the same table with each other; but all this wrangling among the Sisters can not go down to the foundation of the unity of the Family, and break that; they are Sisters still, (God made them so,) though they do not speak to each other. The boughs and branches of the one organic Catholic tree may be tossed by the winds of mutual discussion and flap against each other, but the tree remains one tree, because all hold by the Catholic Sacraments to Christ.

Catholic Sacraments, I say. There may be beautiful ordinances, but there are no Catholic Sacraments without the Apostolic Ministry. The Anglican Apostolic succession of Orders prior to 1617, cannot be impeached by Rome; though heretofore, that is to say before the Pope was declared infallible, it was absolutely vital to her position to impeach them if possible; by foul means, if she could not by fair. But even if there had been forty thousand irregularities in that succession prior to 1617, at that date, at any rate, Mark A. De Dominis, Roman Catholic Archbishop of Spalato, went to England, and, joining with the Archbishop of Canterbury and the Bishops of London and Ely, consecrated George Monteigne and Nicholas Felton to be Bishops; and there is not to-day a single Anglican Bishop, Priest or Deacon in all the world, that cannot trace his Orders directly to Monteigne and Felton, from them to Mark A. De Dominis, and so directly into the Roman succession itself. So that if Rome's Orders and Sacraments are valid, ours are equally so. The two stand or fall together.

Permit me to quote here a somewhat lengthy, but pertinent passage from Ffoulkes's late letter to Archbishop Manning.

"My Lord," he says, " you have preceded me, yourself, in expatiating on the workings of the Holy Spirit in the Church of England with your accustomed eloquence, and have not hesitated to attribute to Its members many graces in virtue of the Sacrament of Baptism, which you allow they administer, on the whole, validly; but there you stop. I feel morally constrained to go further still. If I had to die for it, I could not possibly subscribe to the idea that the Sacraments to which I am admitted week after week in the Roman Communion—Confession and the Holy Eucharist, for instance—confer any graces, any privileges, essentially different from what I used to derive from those same Sacraments, frequented with the same dispositions, in the Church of England. On the contrary, I go so far as to say, that comparing one with another strictly, some of the most edifying communions that I can remember in all my life, were made in the Church of England, and they were administered to me by some that have since submitted to be re-ordained in the Church of Rome; a ceremony, therefore, which, except as qualifying them to undertake duty *there*, I must consider superfluous. Assuredly, so far as the registers of my own spiritual life carry me, I have not been able to discover any greater preservatives from sin, any greater incentives to holiness, in any that I have received since; though in saying this, I am far from intending any derogation to the latter. I frequent them regularly; I prize them exceedingly; I have no fault to find with their administration or their administrators in general. All that I was ever taught to expect from them they do for me, due allowance being made for my own short-comings. Only, I cannot possibly subscribe to the notion of my having been a stranger to their beneficial effects till I joined the Roman Communion. And I deny that it was my faith alone that made them what they were to me before then, unless it is through my faith alone that they are what they are to me now. Holding, myself, that there are realities attaching to the Sacraments of an objective character, I am persuaded, and have been more and more confirmed in this conviction as I have grown older, that the Sacraments administered in the Church of England are realities, objective realities, to the same extent as any that I could now receive at your hands; so that you yourself, therefore, consecrated the Eucharist as truly, when you were Vicar of Leamington, as you have ever done since. This may or may not be your own belief. But you shall be one of my foremost witnesses to its credibility, for I am far from basing it on the experiences of my own soul.

"My Lord, I have always been accustomed to look upon the Sacraments as so many means of grace, and to estima'e their value not by the statements of theologians, but by their effects on myself, my neighbors and mankind at large. And the vast difference between the moral tone of society in the Christian and the pagan worlds, I attribute not merely to the superiority of the rule of life prescribed in the Gospels, but to the inherent grace of the Sacraments enabling and assisting us to keep it to the extent we do. Taking this principle for my guide, I have been engaged constantly, since I joined the Roman Communion, in instituting comparisons between members of the Church of England and members of the Church of Rome generally, and between our former and our present selves in particular; or between Christianity in England and on the Continent; and the result in each case has been to confirm me in the belief, which I have already expressed, that the notion of the Sacraments exercising any greater influence upon the heart and life in the Church of Rome than in the Church of England, admitting the dispositions of those who frequent them to be the same in both cases, is preposterous. * * * * What I have seen of Roman Catholics myself, since joining their church, all points to the same conclusion. Till then I knew them only by report; which, founded on prejudice, was far from being in their favor; and I was horrified to find how shamefully it had misrepresented them. I found them—I mean the educated classes—all that in general estimate, members of a Christian church should be; God-serving, charitable, conscientious, refined, intelligent; and I could discern nothing idolatrous or superstitious in their worship, not anything at variance with first principles in their daily life. At home or abroad I was equally surprised to find them so different from what my traditional informants had described them; with so much to admire where I had supposed there was so much to reprobate. But afterwards, when my first emotions consequent on this discovery had subsided, when I came to ask myself the question, are these then the only true Christians that you have ever known in your life; and till you conversed with them, had you never conversed with a true Christian before? I can scarely describe the recoil it occasioned in me! Why my own father and mother would have compared with the best of them in all the virtues ordinarily possessed by Christians living in the world and discharging their duties conscientiously towards

God and their neighbors, in, through, and for Christ. * * *
Then I have had relatives and friends, in numbers, members of the Church of England, whose homes I will undertake to say are, to all intents and purposes, as thoroughly Christian as any to be found elsewhere; and it would be sheer affectation or hypocrisy in me, were I to pretend the contrary; or else to claim for my own friends and relatives any peculiar excellence distinguishing them from average specimens of the Anglican body. For a calm, unpresuming, uniform standard of practical christianity, I have seen nothing as yet amongst ourselves in any country superior to that of the English parsonage and its surroundings. Go where I will, I am always thrown back upon one of these as the most perfect ideal of a Christian family; a combination amongst its members of the highest intelligence with the most unsullied purity and earnest faith I ever witnessed on earth.

"If it be said that faith and integrity of purpose make members of the Church of England what they are without the Sacraments in mature life, by what argument, I should like to know, can it be proved that it is not to their faith and integrity of purpose solely that members of the Roman Catholic Church are indebted likewise for all the progress they make? The only test of the efficaciousness of the Sacraments appreciable by common sense lies in their influence upon conduct. If, therefore, it were capable of proof, as distinct from assertion, which it is not, both that all the Sacraments administered in the Church of England save one, were shams, and all administered in the Church of Rome were without exception realities, how comes it that we are not incomparably more exalted characters ourselves than we were formerly, or that Roman Catholic countries on the Continent are not incomparably more penetrated to the core with Christianity than England?"

This gift of Sacramental unity to Catholicity is

divine. And so long as the Apostolic Ministry and Sacraments continue, man cannot destroy the unity that God makes through them, any more than man can destroy a particle of matter. Men may, indeed, do acts towards each other that are inconsistent with it; but that will be fallible man's inconsistency with what God has done, not man's destruction of what God has done. For let us advance a step, if you please.

This divine gift of unity requires of us, of course, a corresponding duty; namely, mutual love and unison of wills among those who are organically one. And the natural expression of this unison of wills and mutual love is intercommunion between all parts of the one Catholic Church. But if, as is unhappily the case, intercommunion is temporarily suspended between the parts of the Church, so that the hundred and seventy millions do not communicate with the hundred millions, the underlying unity coming from the action of God, that binds them together into one Catholic Church, is neither forfeited nor broken.

The hundred millions of Old Catholics, Greeks, Russo-Greeks, Georgians, Armenians, Alt-Catholics and Anglicans, hold that Rome's exclusive claim to be the whole Church, is not only a most pregnant error, fraught with untold evils, but also an exhibition of the most stupendous arrogance and pride. There is positively no warrant for it either in Scripture or in history. The sacramental theory has warrant in both.

It has warrant in Scripture; for saith St. Paul touching the Sacrament of Baptism, "For as the body is one and hath many members, and all the members of that one body being many, are one body; so also is Christ. *For by one spirit we are all baptized into one body.*" And saith St. Paul again, touching the Eucharist, "The bread which we break, is it not the Communion of the Body of Christ? *For we being many are one bread and one body, for we are all partakers of that one bread.*" In both these passages the *cause* of the unity is declared to be the Sacraments, "*For* we are all baptized into one body." "We are one bread and one body. *For* we are all partakers of that one bread." Again to the Galatians, "For as many of you as have been baptized into Christ have put on Christ, for ye are all one in Christ Jesus." But where in Scripture is there a passage declaring that the organic unity of the Church is created in any other, and antagonistic way? The Scripture indeed, hav'ng set up the Sacramental unity of the Catholic

Church, could not declare also an antagonistic theory of unity without stultifying Itself.

This sacramental theory has warrant too in history as well as in Scripture. For the exclusive theory of Rome was resisted from the time it made its first faint appearance in the Catholic Church until to-day. In the early centuries the whole Eastern part of the Catholic Church would not listen to it an instant. As it grew in strength and insolence during the darkest time of the Middle Ages, the whole Eastern or Greek part of the Catholic Church, at that time by far the largest, most enlightened and numerous part, with the Patriarch of Constantinople at its head, rose and excommunicated the Bishop of Rome and all his adherents. Thus four out of the five great Patriarchates of the world cut off the one Western or Roman Patriarchate. The Roman theory then, left to itself, easily gained additional strength and self-assertion in the West, until in the sixteenth century the Catholic part of the church in England could endure it no longer. On it went increasing, until in the nineteenth century the German, French, and Swiss Alt-Catholics could bear the strain not another day. So the Roman part of the Church cut itself off first from the whole Eastern part of the church, then from the Anglican, and then from the Alt-Catholic part. And the Vatican, forsooth, with its Protestant theory of unity, sits oblivious, with a kind of self-conscious innocence, among these turmoils of the centuries which it hath introduced into the Catholic Church. So a man brings powder into a fair and stately mansion, blows it up, and then sits down in one miserable torn room and goes off into a revery on the loveliness of a whole and unharmed mansion. Protestantism, whether outside of Rome, or sitting crowned with the tiara on the Papal throne itself, is, indeed, not a life and an organizer but a disorganizer and a death.

The Pope of Rome, although he does not by any means reach back into the earlier centuries of the life of the Catholic Church, is yet an individual of some considerable length. And it certainly is not an edifying spectacle to find him forgetting to-day what he said yesterday about this very matter of Sacramental unity. To-day, since the Vatican Decree of Infallibility, it is Rome alone that is the Catholic Church; but yesterday, that is to say, in the thirteenth century, Pope Gregory Xth, in summoning the Council of Florence, at which an attempt was made to heal the difficulty between the Greek or Eastern and the Latin or Western parts of the Church, uses this language concerning the Catholic Church, namely: "Because of our extreme bitterness in beholding *the rent of the Catholic Church foreshadowed in the net* of Peter, the fisherman, that *brake* for the multitude of fishes it enclosed ; we do not say divided as regards Its Faith * * *but notoriously and lamentably divided as regards Its faithful members.*" To-day, it is Rome alone that is the Catholic Church ; but yesterday, that is to say, in the fifteenth century, Pope Eugenius IVth said to his envoys, "It is for the *union* of the Eastern and Western Church, so long and so ardently desired by us, that you are sent ;" or, as he told the Greek Catholics, when he despaired of such restoration of intercommunion, "In what shall we be benefited if we fail to *unite* the *Church of God.*" Ah, instead of claiming, then, that Rome alone is the Catholic Church, he asserts that the Catholic Church of God included other Communions besides Rome, the four other Patriarchates besides his own ; and that, instead of its being true that whosoever was not in communion with him was out of the Catholic Church, he admits that he himself was not in communion with the whole Catholic Church. In the fifteenth century, at any rate, he included in the Catholic Church of God, as Anglicans do to-day, the Old Catholics of that time, who stood stiffly against him for the ancient constitution of that Church.

Indeed Ffoulkes, himself at the time a Roman Catholic, writing before the decree of Infallibility, says as follows: viz., "The formal teaching of the Popes, ever since the rupture (*i. e.* between the Greek Catholics and the Roman Catholics,) has been that the church is divided *as regards her members;* and that there are Churches forming part of the Catholic Church which are, and have been for ages, out of communion with the Roman See * * * * They most unquestionably have conceded that what we call the Roman Catholic Church has not constituted the whole Church; and that they themselves have not spoken at the head of the whole Church since the rupture between the Greek and Roman parts of Catholicity." "Furthermore," continues this Roman Catholic writer, "as one of the most warmly debated points in modern times has been the power of the Popes and their true relation to the Church, who can fail to be struck with the absence of any formal assertion on their part that the terms 'Catholic' and 'Roman Catholic' are strictly convertible; with the fact that they have never striven to appropriate the term 'Catholic,' pure and simple, to their own Communion, but have commonly called it themselves, and been content that it should be called by others, the Roman Catholic Church as being its strict and adequate title." In accordance with this, what says the Creed of Pius, according to which every pervert to Rome has to pronounce his profession of faith? "I, N— N—, with a firm faith, believe and profess all and every one of those things which are contained in that creed, which the Holy Roman Catholic Church maketh use of." The Missal, too, is called not the Catholic, but the Roman Missal. Mr. Ffoulkes continues : "Where, indeed, is the part of Christendom seriously purporting to call itself *The Catholic Church* in these days? Roman Catholic, Anglo-Catholic, Orthodox Eastern, all in their degree seem influenced by some hidden spell to abstain from arrogating to themselves or attributing to each other the Epithet "Catholic" without qualification, as it is applied to the Church in the Creed."

However, gentlemen, this was written by a Roman Catholic prior to 1870. But since it was written, the Pope has been declared infallible; and that has changed matters with Rome very much. The decree of Papal Infallibility rids her of a load of troubles she formerly had. In order to relieve herself of the fearful charge, and fact too, of being not only an openly schismatical body in England, but also heretical as violating provisions of the First Six General Councils, it has heretofore, I repeat, been of vital importance to her to impeach, if not by fair then by foul means, the validity of Anglican orders. The position of the Greek Catholic Church, whose faith and orders it had not been vital to her to impugn, was nevertheless another ugly and unanswerable fact against her. But no matter for all this now. Since the Vatican decree, and according to that decree, Rome solely is the whole Church; and every thing else, however Catholic it may have been before, is to her a mere sect. For since that decree no unimpeachability on the head of orthodoxy, of valid orders, of jurisdiction, or of practical working, any longer makes the least difference to her. She, with her now infallible Pope, claiming to be the only Christian Church, can enter upon the jurisdiction of any non-papal Bishop, whether Anglican or Greek, and set up her Episcopal Thrones as the only Thrones having Christian authority. The Pope with one plunge of his spurs up to their rowels has sent the Roman steed, at least in its own estimation, bounding clear out of all ugly facts of the past and present, in which it had been tumbling entangled. Rome is in the serio-comic attitude of one who, finding that History overturns her claims, leaps away from History. However, the past is nevertheless secure; and History is a sad tell-tale, and an invincible advocate. And as Rome thus bounds away from it all, the hundred millions gaze at her act with sorrow, not unmingled with quiet, courteous, but triumphant mirth. The Patriarch of Rome had reached a point, under the developments of hostile discussion, where he was compelled to break either with Romanism or with History.

Ah, what a dream of the distraught it is, for Rome to imagine for an instant that she can turn aside God's Hand from its work, that she can shut off the action of His own appointed Sacraments as they go forth to bind men into organic unity with His Christ and with each other; that she can smite that unity as with a painted wooden sword, and, by her Protestant theory, that the mere concord of men's intellects can make a one organic Church, or their mere discord break It, sunder what God Himself hath united. If Protestantism is the sin of essential adultery, Romanism is the essential sin of divorce.

But this argument of Catholicity's touching the Sacramental unity of the Church is not yet quite fully developed. For were it taken without any qualification whatever, it would be incomplete and prove too much. There is something else to be said as to discord of mind in the Church, or all in the Church were left in utter confusion.

Most decidedly, a heretic, one who presumes to deny anything that God Himself speaks in the Creed, forfeits the Sacraments. And most decidedly, on that forfeiture, Christ i. e., God, Who makes the Sacramental unity of the Church, hath the power and the right to break what *He* hath made, by excommunicating the heretic.

But the outward visible part, or Body of Christ, through which He acts, is the Catholic Church; it is not the Pope alone that is Christ's Body Mystical.

Now for *Christ*, thus through the Catholic Church, His Body, to cut off a heretic from Its unity, because that heretic will not submit to what God has said, is one thing; but for the *Bishop of Rome*, who surely is not Jesus Christ, acting clearly at his own instance, to attempt to cut a man off because that man will not submit to *his* views, uttered on his own responsibility from time to time, and, in the language of the Infallibility Decree, "not because of the consent of the rest," even of the Roman part "of the Church," is quite another, and a very different thing.

Were the Pope the Vicar of Christ, were the whole

Catholic Church summed up in the Pope, were he, as he stands in the Vatican, the incarnation, the visible presence of God, the Body of God on Earth, then his excommunication would, of course, be Christ's action. But Catholicity hath denied and resisted these Papal claims from their very first appearance. We shall prove by and by that these claims are baseless. No, it is the Church that is the incarnation of Christ on Earth, and not the Pope. And as it was Christ and not the Pope that made the Sacramental unity of the Church, so it is Christ alone in His Church, and not the Pope, that has power to break an individual or a body of individuals away from it.

The *whole* Church, that is to say Christ, hath excommunicated Protestantism. But the Roman communion has not been excommunicated by the whole Church, but only by the Greek *part* of the Church. It is therefore not excommunicated from Catholicity at all. And the Greek Church has not been excommunicated by the *whole* church, but only by the Roman part of the Church; the Greek Church is therefore not excommunicated from Catholicity at all. And so of the Anglican and Alt-Catholic Communions. Herein then is seen the difference between the divisions of the Catholic Church and the utter separation of all Protestant sects from the Catholic Church. The latter are schismatic bodies; the different parts of the Catholic Church are not in schism, but are suffering under the evils of a disruption of Catholic concord.

But, you will say, suppose now, that when Christ in his Catholic Church has cut off a heretic, that heretic carries away with him the Apostolic Orders and Sacraments; what then? Ah, gentlemen, let history answer. When *Christ* has cut off, He has invariably brought to naught a really heretical sect, notwithstanding its Sacraments. History's answer is, It is hopeless thus to attempt to defeat *God* by carrying away the Sacraments. Where are the Arians, the Pelagians, the Apollinarians, the Macedonians, the Nestorians, the Eutychians, and innumerable bodies that went off with the orders, some of those bodies of vast size too? God speedily ended them; and their very names are strange to our ears.

But compare such rapid death and oblivion of what God hath cut off, with the unharmed and continuous life and vigor through the ages of what the Pope alone has tried to cut off, if you would have a commentary upon a real excommunication from the Catholic Church, in contrast with an excommunication which is a mere sham and travesty. Behold the vast Greek Catholic Church with its thousand years of mighty life, and its enormous growth and vigor since the separation between the East and West; behold, too, the Anglican Catholic Church. A sect, from the time it is cut off from the Catholic Church, never recovers; it withers; its career is always downwards to death. But the Anglican Church shows that it has the Catholic life. For even after having been overwhelmed with Protestants in pulpit, Episcopal Throne, Theological Seminary, and pew, she is nevertheless recovering; for she is rooted in the Catholic Tree; and against no part of the Catholic Church can the gates of Hell prevail.

FIFTH CONFERENCE.

CONSTITUTION OF THE CHURCH, IN ITS PRIESTLY, SACRIFICIAL, PROPHETIC, AND REGAL FUNCTIONS, ACCORDING TO CATHOLICITY. THE CHURCH'S GOVERNMENT EPISCOPAL, NOT PAPAL. GALLICANISM, A LOGICAL MISTAKE. HIERARCHY WITHIN THE EPISCOPATE. PAPAL SUPREMACY NOT SUSTAINED BY SCRIPTURE.

GENTLEMEN,

A second fundamental issue between Catholicity and Romanism is this, namely: Catholicity claims that Romanism is the slow but stubborn development of an absolute monarchy in the Latin part of the Church, unknown to early days, and the prolific mother of many other deviations from Catholicity. The efforts of Rome to alter the government of the Church from Episcopal to Papal, have been resisted by the rest of the Church from the first. The entire contest between Catholicity and Romanism has not really changed since it began. But since the Vatican decree of 1870, it has been practically narrowed to the above single issue. For, if the Papal Supremacy be right, the entire Catholic Church must, of course, accept it; and, with it, all the rest of Romanism. The Papal Supremacy is, therefore, the fortress of Rome's position. If that stands, she stands; if that falls, the war is over.

When the Bishop of Rome sent letters to the Patriarch of Constantinople, inviting him to attend the late Vatican Council in 1870, in declining the invitation for himself and his brother Bishops, and declining to open, or even to lift from the table where the papal delegates had placed it, the elegant case in which the invitation was enclosed, the venerable Patriarch expressed in the following words the fixed attitude of all parts of the Catholic Church not in communion with the Papal see, viz:

"Since it is manifest that there was a Church in existence ten centuries ago, Which held the same doctrines in the east as in the west, in the Old as in the New Rome, let us each recur to that; and see which of us has added aught, which has diminished aught therefrom. And let all that may have been added be struck off, if any there be, and whatever it be; and let all that has been diminished therefrom be re-added, if any there be, and whatever it be. And then we shall all, unawares, find ourselves united in the same symbol of Catholic Orthodoxy."

In a similar strain, and with almost identical language, did the Patriarch of Alexandria also reply to the Roman messengers that conveyed a like invitation to him and to his brother Bishops. He declined communion with the see of Rome, and with all churches adhering to that see; and he declined even meeting in council with them, till the Pope should recede from his usurpations. All was courteous and diplomatic, for each eastern Patriarch received formally, and in full Canonicals, the messengers of the Patriarch of Rome, but all was politely firm.

In the investigation of this vital issue between Catholicity and Romanism, let me first present to you the ancient constitution of the Church according to Catholicity; after which we will view the radically different autocracy which Rome has succeeded in imposing on her adherents, and which she insists that the rest of the Catholic Church shall accept. We begin, then, with the Catholic theory.

Jesus Christ is four-fold; He is Priest, Sacrifice, Prophet, and King. First, then, according to Catholicity, there is but one Priest, Jesus Christ. He alone can offer a Sacrifice; He alone can forgive sins.

Now one purpose for which He is here within the

visible Catholic Church is to act as Priest. But if, as Priest He had remained invisible, His Priestly Function would not have adapted itself to the conditions of time and space, nor to the wants of those who are in the Church of time and space. To make Himself accessible to us as the sole Priest, He must break out into Priestly visibility. He takes to Himself therefore, a special visible Priestly Body within the Church.

Now if the Catholic Church consisted of but one small parish, He need only have taken to Himself a single earthly Priest for an outward visible Body, through which His Priestly Function could act. But as the earth is extensive, His Priestly Function, on striking its medium and becoming visible, breaks up into many earthly Priests, for the manifold distribution and practical application of itself all round the globe. Thus it is that the One Priest is enabled audibly to pronounce the words of pardon and of blessing, of oblation and of consecration, every where simultaneously. Nevertheless, all these earthly Priests form, after all, only one organic Body; a single Body that has a manifold presence in the Church; a single Body the Soul of which is the Priestly Function of Jesus Christ. For each separate earthly Priest is but a reiteration, on account of the conditions of space, of every other Priest, as "one only of innumerable shadows cast by the same object." Being reiterations of each other, Catholic Priests are all equal. Then, in this one Body of the earthly Priesthood, in order to avoid differences in action, and the conflicts, which the actual multiplicity of Priests on earth would occasion, certain ecclesiastical regulations have from the first been observed, restraining each Priest to a local district. In short, in like manner as Christ stands in the world, *God* incarnate in the Great Body of the Church, so He stands within the Church itself, *a Priest*, yea rather *the Priest* incarnate and visible in the great one Sacerdotal Body, an incarnation within an incarnation, a visible body within a visible body.

Every earthly Priest, therefore, holds his power to exercise Priestly functions not from his Bishop, but directly from God. He preaches, offers the Sacrifice, baptises, and pardons, in virtue of the power which the Holy Ghost has given to him. The Bishop is, indeed, the superior and the pastor of the Priest, but the Priest is not a simple vicar of the Bishop. To claim that he is, is to take a first step towards Romanism. Men, though they may be channels through which power comes, are never the source whence it comes. It is Christ in His Church that is this source. And

Christ, through His instrument the Bishop, gives the Sacerdotal power directly to the Priest at Ordination. Rome, on the other hand, claims that the plenitude of all power is in the Pope; that the Bishops are merely vicars of the Pope, and the Priests merely vicars of the Bishops.

Secondly. As there is but one Priest, so there is but one Sacrifice, Jesus Christ. As He is a "Priest forever," the Apostle tells us "it is of necessity" that He should "have somewhat to offer" forever. Being, then, the one Priest in Heaven and on earth, He pleads His one Sacrifice simultaneously in Heaven and on earth before the Father. On the Heavenly Altar He ever stands, "The Lamb as It had been slain." This great and perpetual Sacrificial transaction of the "Priest forever," on striking the medium of space and time, adapts itself to the conditions of space and time. Like His Priesthood it, too, breaks out into visibility in the visible Church.

Now if the Church consisted of but one small parish, there would be needed but one visible Altar and one visible Eucharistic Sacrifice for the realization to us of the one great perpetual Sacrificial transaction of Jesus Christ. But, as before, the earth is extensive. When, therefore, Christ's act, as He perpetually displays His glorious wounds before God the Father, strikes the medium of space and time, it breaks out into the many Altars of space and the repeated Eucharists of time, in order to meet, by manifold distribution, the wants of that part of the one Church which is subject to the conditions of extended space and of continuous time.

I do not know how it is with you, gentlemen, but to my faith the distinctions that are drawn between Christ's own Body in Heaven and Christ's Sacramental Body on earth, as though they were in some mysterious way two separate existences, the one immovable in an astronomic Heaven and the other movable and coming through space to the earth, are incomprehensible jargon. They are born of the Continental Reformation; they are a logical denial of the unity of the Church Militant and Triumphant; they suppose Eternity to be simply a very long Time, instead of something essentially different from Time; and they suppose Heaven to be a very far and very fair portion of space, instead of something supernatural, and essentially different from space. Church Militant and Triumphant, instead of occupying two separate portions of space quite distant from each other, is a One Body, existing, however, under two conditions. It stands, as a whole, in the immediate Presence of God the Father; It is, as such undivided Body, standing in the Presence of God the Father, at once within space and not within space; It exists equally in Time with its conditions and in Eternity with its different conditions; It is at the same time visible and invisible. Its Priest and and Its Sacrifice exist, therefore, under the same two conditions; within space, namely, and not within space, in Time and also in Eternity. Its Sacrifice is therefore, at once invisible because it exists within the Heavenly conditions, and visible because it exists within the earthly conditions, these differing conditions not dividing the one Sacrifice. So that, after all, at all the Altars, all over the earth, and all through time, it is not many separate Eucharists, many separate Sacrifices. No, it is all one only Food; one only everflowing Blood; one perpetual Eucharist, one single perpetual Sacrifice, Jesus Christ. Thus all the combined earthly Altars, though many, are after all one only Altar standing at once in Heaven and on earth; and moreover, as such Altar, they all form simply the one visible part of the Heavenly Altar, as inseparable from It as a body is from its soul. So that when we look at our earthly Altar, we are merely looking at an outward and visible part of the great alone Altar of the great alone Priest, whereon He stands, both visible and invisible, "The Lamb as it had been slain." If I may be permitted a figure to make the idea perhaps clearer; though our earthly Altars are many, yet they stand, so to speak, all round an unbroken circumference, the common center of which is the Heavenly Altar where The Lamb is. So that when we each kneel before and gaze at our earthly Altar, in whatever church, we are all adoring with the angels and looking in directly, and as through a circumference of lenses, each upon the same Heavenly Altar at the common centre of the whole circle, where stands our Sacrifice and our God, Who, for our sake in space and time, comes out into Sacrificial visibility all round the circumference. Thus the God-man, whom we behold and adore at our several earthly Altars, is the God-man Who is on the Heavenly Altar; and in adoring Him *at* our earthly Altars we are adoring Him *on* the Heavenly Altar; for we of the Church Militant are as much in the Presence of God the Father, as are the angels of Heaven.

Permit me to say here, parenthetically, even though it be extraneous to the current of our present thought, a word or two touching a difficulty that may have presented tself to your minds. Catholicity, you will say, declares that the Sacrifice presented before the Father at Its Altars is the Body of Christ; and yet It also declares that the Church is the Body of Christ; and is there not here an inconsistency? But the mental hesitancy, into which these two statements throw the non-catholic mind, clears itself away at once, when we consider the absolute unity of Christ, and the unity of His action. For, He is the One Priest offering Himself as the One Sacrifice. If we are to join Him in pleading that Sacrifice, we must become a part of Him; otherwise it would not be Himself offering Himself, His Body offering His Body. Thus He is the Church as Offerer, and He is at the same time the Eucharist as the Thing offered. The apparent inconsistency grows inevitably out of the marvelous fact that Christ is both Priest and Victim. Thus, to deny that the Catholic Church is the Body of Christ, must end logically in the Unitarian denial that Christ is both Priest and Victim.

Thirdly. Our Lord is also Prophet, that is to say Teacher. For, as a Prophet is one who states the underlying truths and laws in accordance with which events happen, he is primarily a teacher, and only subordinately a foreteller. When this Teaching Function of our Lord strikes the medium of space and time, it likewise comes out into visibility within the Church, breaking into many visible earthly preachers for the manifold distribution and practical application of itself to all parts of the earthly Church. So that the combined Catholic pulpits are the one outward Body of the one Teacher, Christ.

Fourthly. But Christ is not only Priest, Sacrifice and Prophet. He is also King, or Ruler. If, as Ruler in the Church, He remained a mere impalpable influence, the invisibility of this Regal power would not only be inconsistent with the visibility of the Church Itself, and of His other functions in It, but it would leave all order to the incertitude of men's differing but honest impressions as to what ought to be done, as each would think he was guided in some mystical, transcendental way aright. Christ would no more have adapted Himself as such Ruler to the conditions of time and space or to the needs of those in the Church of time and space, than He would if He had remained invisible as a Priest, or as a Sacrifice, or as a Teacher. No, all is harmonious. His Church Catholic is a complete and consistent system. His Ruling Prerogative, therefore, on strik ing the medium of time and space, comes out also into visibility.

If the Church were only one small diocese, His Ruling Function would need for its outward earthly body through which to act, one earthly Bishop only. But, again, the earth is extensive. Christ's Ruling Prerogative, therefore, on striking its medium, adapts itself to the conditions of space, by breaking into many Bishops, for the manifold distribution and application of itself within the Church all round the world.

Now just here is the root idea of the Episcopal government of the Catholic Church as opposed to the Papal autocratic government. For, as there is in the Church but one Priest visible and invisible, Jesus Christ, so there is in the Church but one King or Bishop visible and invisible. All the earthly Bishops together form the one visible organic Kingly Body, of which the inward and inseparable living Soul is the Ruling Function of Christ. For each separate earthly Bishop is but a reiteration, on account of the conditions of space, of every other Bishop, as one of "innumerable shadows cast by the same" Kingly object; and, being reiterations of each other, they are all equal. Every Bishop, therefore, holds his power to exercise episcopal functions, not from the Pope, but directly from Christ.

It is in the Combined Episcopate, then, all over the world, that we have the One Bishop, Christ, standing everywhere visible to us as King; just as in the combined Priesthood we have the one Priest, Christ, standing everywhere visible as Priest. It is in the Combined Episcopate, then, that we have the Vicar of Christ on earth, and not in any single one of the Bishops. For the single Bishop of Rome to set himself up, regardless of all the rest, as the alone Vicar of Christ, is a tremendous deviation from the Apostolic constitution of the Church. It is to destroy that Regal Body on earth in which the great Ruler, Christ, stands visible as Ruler everywhere throughout the Church. It is treason and Regicide. It puts a usurper on the throne in place of Jesus Christ's own royal Body. It is an attempt to change most radically the government of the whole Church from Episcopal to Papal.

You will see at a glance, for truth is always consistent with itself, that the Great General Councils of all the Bishops, which for centuries and centuries convened as the undoubted ultimate courts of appeal, were inconsistent with the modern theory that ultimate appeals rest in the Pope. You will see that those General Councils followed harmoniously, and naturally, and truthfully, from the original government of the Catholic Church by the Combined Episcopate.

Indeed Gregory Great, twelve centuries ago, far from putting himself above the Combined Episcopate, said that he honored Ecumenical Councils equally with the four Gospels. And Leo III, in the eighth century, assured the Frankish Bishops when they came to him, that, far from setting himself above the Fathers of the Council of 381, who made additions to the Nicene Creed, he did not venture to put himself on a par with them; and, therefore, would not presume to make the addition to the creed which those Frankish Bishops suggested. Consider, too, these words of the oath which the Popes pronounced on the day of their inauguration for centuries; "I promise to honor and to venerate faithfully the Holy General Councils, to teach that which they have taught, to observe that which they have decreed, and to condemn with heart and mouth that which they have condemned." St. Augustine says that a plenary Council always remains as final arbiter to annul any sentence of any, even the greatest Bishop. Pope Sylvester II. says, " If the Pope listens not to the Church, he ought to be treated as a heathen man and a publican." Pope Leo, in addressing the fathers of the Fourth General Council, A. D. 451, uses the following language, viz: "As the very Christian Emperor has wished an Episcopal Council *to the end that error may be abolished* by a *more authorized judgment*, I have sent my brother Julian, Bishop, Renatus, Priest, and my brother Hilary, Deacon, who will represent me at the Council, and, by a sentence common with you, will establish that which will be pleasing to the Lord." Surely here St. Leo rests the final authority in an Ecumenical Council. Again, the Robber Council of Ephesus had been held, sustaining Eutyches. Thereupon the Pope urged upon the Emperor the summoning of a new Council that should be truly Ecumenical. Theodocius, deceived, and believing that the canonical rules had been observed at the Robber Council, did not wish to consent to a new Council; "Because," said he, " after the solemn decision of the Council, it is not possible to resort to a new judgment." Surely the demand of St. Leo and the refusal of the Emperor prove that both of them rested the final authority in a truly General Council. The Fifth Council in 553, uses, moreover the following language : "There is no other means (except by a General

Council) of knowing the truth in the Faith. Each has need of the aid of his brother, following the Scripture, 'Where two or three are met together,'" etc. This Council judged and condemned Pope Vigilius as a heretic. The sixth General Council, in 680, anathematized Pope Honorius for being a heretic. In 768 Pope Constantine II was deposed by a Council. At the Eighth Council, in 869, after the letters of Pope Nicholas were read, the legates asked of the Council, at the end of its fifth session, "What does the Council say of the things it has just heard? Is this letter canonical or not?" The Council replied, "It is conformable to the canons, it is regular." This, too, is evidence that the Pope deferred to the Council.

Here, then, in the long course of nine centuries, we behold the supremacy of Councils. The law of the Church is the decision of the Combined Episcopate. In the first eight Councils each Bishop writes the phrase " Definiens subscripsi." It is not till we come to the Roman Lateran Councils that the phrase, " Sacro approbante concilio," makes its appearance.

But, furthermore, the very struggles of the Popes in later centuries to rise superior to the dicta of even a Roman Council, is a standing and unanswerable argument that this claim of Papal Supremacy is novel,

When, in the ninth century, the whole Latin Church was excommunicated for its errors by the rest of the Catholic Church, still the idea of the supreme power of the Combined Episcopate in General Council assembled so lingered even in this Latin part, that Pope Gregory XIIth himself appealed to a General Council, as " that, by which and in which the acts of a Pope are accustomed to be judged." The Latin Council of Constance as late as 1414, having summoned John XXIII, deposed him, and afterwards Benedict XIII, also, from the Papacy. Vienne judged Boniface VIII. At its Fifth session the Council of Constance passed the following decree, viz : " The sacred synod of Constance, making a General Council, legitimately assembled to the glory of Almighty God for the extirpation of schism and for the union, and the reformation of the Church in Its Head and in Its members, wishing to execute more easily, more surely, more abundantly, and more freely this union and this reformation, orders, defines, discerns and decrees as follows : This Council, legitimately assembled in the Holy Ghost, making a General Council, and repre senting the Catholic Church, *holds immediately from Jesus Christ a power*, which every person of whatever condition and dignity he may be, *even papal*, is obliged to obey in that which concerns the Faith, the extirpation of the present schism and the reformation of the Church in Its Head and in Its members. Whoever, of whatever condition or dignity he may be, even papal, shall refuse obstinately to obey the statutes, ordinances and precepts, that this Holy Council, or any other legitimate Council assembled, has made, or shall make, upon the aforesaid matters, or upon any thing which regards them, if he does not repent, shall be punished as he deserves; and there shall be employed against him, if it be necessary, other lawful means." The Council of Basle also declared that, as the Church had through Councils frequently deposed Popes when convicted of errors in faith, while no Pope had ever pretended to condemn the Church, the superiority of a Council over a Pope was clear. In short the struggle, even in the Latin part of the Church after the rupture between the East and the West, between its own Councils and its Pope as to which was supreme, continued with shifting successes until at last it is only in modern days that the Gallican School has gone down, and Papal Supremacy over a Council has finally succeeded in setting itself up. Who shall claim, then, that the Papal Supremacy is not a modern fiction? In the Council of Florence, in 1438, Bessarion, an eminent Greek, perhaps the most learned and illustrious of all the Greeks present, said, "We know the rights and privileges of the Roman Church; but we know, also, that these rights have limits. Whatever may be the power of the Roman Church, it is less than that of the General Council and of the Universal Church."

Indeed, gentlemen, show me in the past thousand years of Catholicity where the rising waves of Papal ambition have beaten, and I will show you where the rock-bound continent of the true Vicar of Christ has always stood in resistance; nay, where the very Rock Himself, Jesus Christ, in His true visible Kingly Body, the Combined Episcopate, has always stood unmoved, dashing back those Papal billows.

Let me say here, incidentally, before I come to the main argument about the Rock, that it is, indeed, absurd on the face of it, absurd *à priori*, absurd at its very first mention, that Christ should have promised to found His Church on a mere man, instead of on the God-Man. It is Protestantism, this founding churches on men; on Calvin, or Peter, or Luther, or Wesley. And, therefore, again, the Pope is simply a superb Protestant clothed in canonicals. Indeed St. Paul, in his celebrated rebuke to the Corinthians, where he says, "Now this I say, that every one of you saith I am of Paul, and I of Apollos, and I of Peter, and I of Christ," makes such very choice of Peter as the one peculiar note and test of Catholic fellowship and of covenant with God, a mark of schism, rather than of Catholicity.

If Anglican Catholics were alone in denying the Papal Supremacy, and all the rest of the Catholic Church were, and had always been against us, we might seem to be setting little stress on the great blessings of Catholic concord and of uninterrupted intercommunion. But let Anglican Catholicity be blotted from the map, what nevertheless is to be done with the great East, with four out of the five great Patriarchates of Catholicity? "Are the unchanged and unchangeable Churches of Asia, of Greece, and of Russia to be taken also out of the history of the world and of the Church?" They have denied from the first, and still do deny, the Papal Supremacy. "When the whole of the East, holding equally with ourselves the great principle of unity, resists, nevertheless, a dogma, which another great portion of the Church enforces as the only condition of communion with Herself, then we are sure the breach rests not with that portion which denies, but with that which asserts so great and unjustifiable a claim "* as the Papal Autocracy.

We have found the true Vicar of Christ not in a single Bishop, but in all the Bishops combined. Now the Romanist charges us with imagining that the Church has no earthly Head. The "Catholic Review" of last week, in an article on the First of these Conferences, repeats this charge. Indeed it is one of the stock fallacies with which Romanists easily confound the ill-instructed Churchman. The charge is not true. The fallacy is this. Because we do not accept the Papal Supremacy, we therefore believe the Catholic Church to be a Headless Church so far as this earth is concerned. This will do for an unwary Protestant, to induce him to pass unwittingly by the very question at issue and into the Roman conclusion; but it will not do for a Catholic. The Romanist can always handle a Protestant with great ease; and the reason why the Romanist is so bitter against what are called Ritualists, is because he cannot move them an inch ; that is to say, if the so-called Ritualist is a true Catholic, and not an Evangelical who is temporarily dancing through a little *mere* Ritualism on his steady way from latitudinarianism to the other ex

* The Rev. W. J. E. Bennett.

treme of Rome. If Catholics are all going to Rome, as is charged by the ignorant, then it is most marvelous that the very points which Catholics hold are the very points which have caused Döllinger and the Alt-Catholics violently to tear themselves away from Rome, in which they were born and reared, which they have loved, and in which they lived, some of them to ripe and grave old age. Such men as Pusey, Liddon, Carter, and the Catholic school generally, refuse to be judged by the case of a few giddy-headed persons, who, waking up to the misery of Protestantism, stagger, dazzled and blinded, away from Low-Churchmanship, caper through a little mere Ritualism, and then tumble over into Rome, enthusiastically sure, superciliously confident, tumultuously certain that they have gotten at the bottom of this prodigious and complicated question that for over a thousand years has divided the Church.

Of course, gentlemen, the Church has a Head. That is not the question at all. But the question is, in what that Head consists ; whether in the Combined Episcopate, or in one only of its Bishops. It is an undeniable fact, and it settles the question, at any rate, between Catholicity and Romanism, beyond all peradventure, that, in the era of the first six great

General Councils, it was the Combined Episcopate alone, and not the Bishop of Rome, that was the ultimate authority and Great Vicar of Christ in questions of faith and of discipline; it is an undeniable historical fact, that nothing doubtful was for centuries settled in the Church, no matter what the Bishop of Rome might say, till the Combined Episcopate spoke in Ecumenical Council.

But let me complete the idea of the Apostolic Constitution of the Catholic Church. You will remember that I stated, while I was speaking of the body of the Priesthood, that, in order to avoid those conflicts which the multiplicity of actual human Priests would otherwise occasion, certain ecclesiastical regulations have, not perhaps from the very first, but from a very early date, been observed, restraining Priests to local districts.

Now carry that same idea over into the Episcopate. You will perceive that, if there were no analogous ecclesiastical regulations for the Episcopate, there could not fail to arise confusions, and collisions in action among the earthly Bishops, owing to their actual multiplicity. And so there have been, not from the very first, but from quite early days, ecclesiastical regulations restraining Bishops to local districts.

Nor is this all. There has been a hierarchy within the Episcopate from very early days; consisting of Bishops, Arch-Bishops, Patriarchs and a Primate as Head of the whole. There is not and never has been the slightest issue between Rome and us about such a hierarchy; and, moreover, the great Anglican Bishops and controversial writers have, with consenting voice, admitted the Primacy of Rome. In fact the Church must have primacies. Every province must have its head; it is the Arch-Bishop, or, as we call him in America, the Senior Bishop. Every Patriarchate or vast Communion like the Anglican must have its head; it is the Patriarch, or, as with us, the Arch-Bishop of Canterbury. And, were intercommunion restored between all parts of the Church, the whole Combined Episcopate must have its chief Primate; and, according to the decrees of the General Councils, that chief Primate would of course be the Bishop of Rome. But the trouble between Catholicity and Romanism arises outside of this, and is two-fold.

For, first, the Bishop of Rome has not been satisfied to rest in his ancient Primacy within the Episcopate, but has striven, instead, to usurp the autocracy over the Episcopate. Instead of being first among equals, he claims, that is to say, to hold the same relative attitude to all Bishops, that any Bishop holds to his Priests. This is virtually an effort to create a fourth order in the Ministry. He claims the appointment of all Bishops; that every cause of moment shall go up to himself; that he shall have the right to suspend, condemn or acquit at his own will; instead of receiving law and faith from the Church, he claims to give the law and the truth to the Church. In short, it is a demand that the legislative, executive and judicial powers in the Church be centered in himself, and that he be responsible to no one. For, the Vatican decree declares that the Pope holds not merely the chief part, but the "entire fulness of the supreme power." Now this is what Catholicity resists.

Let us take an illustration. We need, for instance a President of the United States. But let any President draw the sword, overthrow the constitution, and usurp the powers of an absolute Oriental Autocrat, let him presume to appoint for each State its Governor, to supervise or repeal its state, county and municipal codes, to reverse, if he please, all decrees of the courts state or federal, and to declare his own irresponsible will to be law for all, and the American citizen or State that would not resist to the end such usurpation, would be traitor to the Federal Constitution, and unworthy the name of American. In the State, better civil war than such submission ; in the Church, better non-intercommunion than a similar submission. No, no ; the Catholic must stand loyal to the original constitution of the Catholic Church, if he would be loyal to that Church. He cannot be loyal at once to the Pope and to the Church; for the Primacy of Rome is one thing ; but the Papal Supremacy is a vastly different thing.

Rome cries to the Greeks and Anglicans, "If you are not Protestants, (and it seems you claim not to be,) yet you are not Catholics. For the Catholic is one who obeys the Pope ; and he who obeys him not is heretic, excommunicated, and, if not a Protestant, he must be an unclassified man." But thus replies one who is a Catholic indeed : "The true Catholic is he who obeys primarily the Church, inasmuch as She exercises the authority which Jesus Christ has conferred upon Her. As to the Pope, because he is the Patriarch of the West, and the first of the other Patriarchs, the true Catholic can obey him on one only condition, that he shall, in his turn, obey as a good Catholic all the laws of the Church. If the Pope transgress these laws, if he violate the constitution established by Christ, if he derogate the Councils of the Church, if he attribute to himself in the name of God a power which he holds neither from God nor from the Church, then he separates himself from the Church. He is no more Chief Primate, but solely chief Disturber. In this case the true Catholic is he who resists him; who appeals to the authority to which the true Primate ought himself to be submissive, viz: the authority of the Church united in a Council really ecumenical."*

Innocent IVth taught, indeed, that one ought not to obey an order of the Pope containing a heresy, or threatening to shake the whole organization of the Church; and that, a Pope being able to fail, it is necessary to say, "I believe that which the Church believes, and not that which the Pope believes." Pius IXth, however, differed with Innocent IVth.

No, the see of Rome, though holding the Primacy, can rightly have no such jurisdictional power as would divide or limit the full power of the Combined Episcopate, which must, according to ancient constitution, remain the supreme earthly Head of the Church. And herein, by the way, consisted the fatal error of the Gallicans. Finding, namely, that, for purposes of

* Michaud.

administrative order, the Church had in the early centuries developed Archbishops, Exarchs and Patriarchs, each with jurisdictional power *within* the Episcopate, the Gallicans went so far as to admit that the chief Primate should himself also have analogous jurisdictional power *over* the whole Episcopate and over the whole Church.

But they failed to see that at this very point the fundamental Apostolic Constitution of the Church was attacked. We must go up in the last resort through the jurisdictional powers of Bishops, Archbishops and Patriarchs to the Kingship of Christ as represented on earth, first by the Board of Apostles to whom He gave all power, and then by the Combined Episcopate as the successors of the Apostles. And we fall into a dissolution of the order of the Apostolic Church, if we go still further up, and over the corpse indeed of the Combined Episcopate, to the Bishop of Rome as the final authority in the Church. This false view of the Primacy has been the logical destruction of Gallicanism. There is indeed no real holding ground between the Papal and the Catholic or Episcopal theories; and Gallicanism, which attempted to stand between the two, was stricken *ab initio* with a mortal disease. Its complete overthrow was only a question of time. After having fatally admitted that the Pope could veto the acts of a General Council, the Gallicans, though historically correct in resisting the further claims of the Pope to supreme autocracy, were logically incorrect. The Jesuits on the other hand, though historically incorrect, were logically correct. The question was, to what shall we go up in the hierarchy as final authority? The Jesuits say, to the Pope; the Catholics say to the Episcopate; but the Gallicans, going as I have said beyond the Catholics, strove to pause at a point below the Jesuits. "Not to the Pope alone," said they, "nor yet to a Council; but to the Pope and a Council." But, alas, though they took a milder view of the Pope than did the Jesuits, they were after all sufficiently Papists; they were to all intents and purposes Romanists and not Catholics; and Romanism is a logical torrent, which will either overwhelm and destroy those who are in it, or will sweep them to its extreme logical conclusions. The Gallican theory was not only weak logically, but impracticable also. Normally it would leave the Church in an inextricable difficulty. For we must have a final deciding court in the Church. Now we can have this either in a Pope or in a General Council. But if this court is to be found in a co-ordination of the Pope and a Council, then, should these two differ from each other, the question on which they differ would be left undetermined, and the Church plunged into confusion. No, the Church can have but one earthly Head. Either the Jesuits or the Catholics are right. It were a monstrosity if It were double-headed. However, Gallicanism is now dead, and probably forever. The Gallicans should have reinforced the Anglicans in the sixteenth century. They have met with their inevitable punishment.

But, as has been said, the trouble between Catholicity and Romanism is two-fold. Secondly, then, Rome not only claims Supremacy over instead of honorary primacy within the Episcopate, but that the Pope is thus supreme "by divine right;" meaning by this phrase, "by Christ's personal appointment." Catholicity denies this. Catholicity admits freely that St. Peter, on account of age and zeal and what we call character, was a man of prominence among the Apostles; freely admits that he had, if you please to call it so, a primacy of honor. This, although not distinctly stated in Scripture, is, nevertheless, possible perhaps to be inferred from Scripture. Indeed there never were twelve men yet, that among them, some were not stronger characters than others, and one the strongest of all. But this is a very different thing from a Primacy of honor in the Church; and a more vastly different thing still from a Primacy of Functions and powers over the Episcopate through all time. Catholicity asserts that even Rome's Primacy of honor in the Church was not of divine appointment or right at all. But that the great and true Vicar of Christ, namely, the Combined Episcopate, after all the Apostles were dead, gave the Primacy of honor to Rome; that it furthermore arranged the hierarchies within Itself, and often rearranged them according to circumstances and to the needs of the Church; creating Patriarchs, and altering the order of precedence among them from time to time. Indeed this is a wise and indispensable condition, considering the length and the exigencies of the centuries of all time. Rome's Primacy was, therefore, entirely of ecclesiastical regulation, and not of divine appointment at all. The ultimate power always continued to lie, and always must lie, in the whole Body of Bishops. Jesus Christ established a single ministry, and this ministry in three Orders, Bishops, Priests and Deacons. And this is the only hierarchy that exists of *Divine* right. And if it is of Divine right, there is nothing that can be superior in the Church to the Episcopate. The Chief Primate comes from the Bishops; the Bishops do not derive their origin from the Pope. The Pope can be Primate, he can be first among the Bishops, without being the source of the Episcopate and Autocrat over all the Bishops. We will see the proof of all this anon, both in Scripture and in history.

Meanwhile I lay down here a fundamental proposition. It is this, namely: if God is a moral Governor, and if each man is a responsible being, then it is simply a logical impossibility for the Popes to have received from God the Supremacy, *i.e.* any such power to coerce men as is claimed, for instance, in the Bull of Paul IV, in the Bull *Unam Sanctam*, and in the Syllabus. For, first, since the Jewish Dispensation closed, and since the cases of Ananias, Sapphira and Elymas, which were exceptional miracles, God refuses to exercise any coercive authority that shall interfere with man's liberty, with his right to live, to think, and to speak. Mr. Baring-Gould develops this idea most admirably in his "Origin and Development of Christianity," and it is to him that I am indebted for it. Now as God refuses to exercise such authority Himself, *He* cannot have transmitted such compulsory authority to any power on earth, whether in State or Church. The divine right of Kings is, therefore, quite as much a fiction as the divine right of the Pope to coerce either heretics or Emperors and their subjects. God exercises moral authority only. He can have transmitted, therefore, directly from Himself, only such moral authority to His Church and to His State as He personally exercises Himself. Any additional authority, either in State or Church, to enforce what is right, must have been conferred not from above downwards, but from below upwards to the government of Church or State by the common consent of the governed, whether in Church or State, and for the purpose of securing and enforcing order among themselves. God only confers from above downwards *moral* authority ; man has the right to confer from below upward coercive or effective authority. The moment, then, the Papal Supremacy is held up as a divine right, it becomes a normal source of confusion and bloodshed ; for it issues inevitably in a conflict between the governed, who assert their inherent rights, and the usurper of coercive powers claimed to be from above, and, therefore, never asked of nor granted by the free consent of the governed.

To complete the idea, then, of the constitution of the Catholic Church. The divine governing grade of Bishops, when correlated together, could not work practically without arranging Primacies within Itself; and could not be prepared to meet the exigencies of all time, without power to rearrange those Primacies at will. Such Primacies are elements of order and sources of strength. But for him who received from the Episcopate the Head Primacy, without, however, any jurisdictional power that would be inconsistent with the full power of the Combined Episcopate, to assume Autocracy over the Episcopate itself was to distort and transform the office that had been bestowed upon him. It was to play the ingrate towards those by whose will he existed as "first among equals." It was to trample the Combined Episcopate under foot. And he stands supreme to-day in a part of the Church against the consent of four out of five of the great Patriarchates of early days and of six out of the seven of modern days; against the decrees of great Roman Councils themselves; and, as we have seen in a previous Conference, against the protest of even living and able Roman Bishops. His ambition has done nothing from the first but disturb the order of the Church, weaken Its Body, and introduce suspension of inter-communion and of co-action among Its members. It led to the sundering of the Easterns from the Westerns in the middle ages; of the Anglicans from the Latins at the Reformation; and to the separation of the Latin part into Old and New Catholics in our own days. Catholicity claims that all that was necessary to the end of organization, order and unity was a general Primate, " a First among equals." Rome claimed that a supreme Pontiff was essential to effect unity. Here is the distinct issue. But was there ever anything more self-convicted of error, than Rome's claim of Supremacy as a necessary condition for unity? For, ever since She set it up, Time has hissed at it, while Christendom has been going to pieces under it. There is in physics, I believe, a substance, which, when you attempt to compress it beyond certain limits, explodes.

The uninstructed or erroneously instructed churchman knows nothing about Rome's Primacy in early days; he simply hates the Pope; and that is all he knows about it. And so Rome, if she can get his ear, is very apt to astonish him by proving to him the Pope's early Primacy. He then does not know where he stands, and is just in condition to be an easy captive to the Papal claim of Supremacy. But the ancient

Primacy, instead of proving Rome's Supremacy of to-day is one of the strongest proofs against it.

Now Rome claims, I repeat, that the Pope as successor of St. Peter is supreme by Christ's personal appointment in Palestine. Let us look at this. There is a preliminary trouble to start with. For even if Christ gave St. Peter the Supremacy, Rome has first to prove that St. Peter, who was Bishop of Antioch, was ever in Rome; which is a doubtful point. It is very remarkable, at any rate, that the courteous St. Paul, in writing to the Romans, should make no allusion to St. Peter, if the latter was Bishop there, but should overrule him by instructing the Romans himself. Secondly; if St. Peter was in Rome, the Romanists have to prove that he ever transferred his see from Antioch to Rome; which is another doubtful point. And, thirdly; that if he did, Christ meant him to transmit his personal authority to his successors. Christ certainly said nothing about that. At any rate, it is strange on the face of it, that the comparatively obscure Linus or Cletus, Bishops of Rome, should have been, in any sense, superior to St. John the Divine, the last living Apostle. However, waive all this. Did Christ personally give St. Peter the Supremacy? Rome says, yes; Catholicity says, nay.

Now one of the three texts on which Rome bases her claim is the text, "Feed my sheep and my lambs." A thought or two on this. What was it? It was a reinstatement of the fallen St. Peter. St. Cyril of Alexandria says, "By the words of our Lord, 'Feed my sheep,' a renewal as it were of the Apostolate, already conferred on him, is understood to take place."

Recall for a moment the incidents that happened just prior to our Lord's death. When, at two o'clock on the morning of Good Friday, Christ was arrested, all the Disciples forsook him. St. Peter particularly had said, but a few hours previously, with his usual warmth, "Though all men should be offended because of Thee, yet will I never be offended; though I should die with Thee, yet will I not deny Thee." He had assured Christ of his love beyond that of the others. All the disciples, indeed, forsook him; but there was something peculiarly flagrant and heinous about St. Peter's case. Christ was led to the High Priest's house. St. Peter returned to watch afar off. While he was warming himself in the palace beneath, one of the maids of the High Priest, looking at him, said, "And thou also wast with Jesus." But he denied, saying, "I know not, neither understand what thou sayest." And he went out into the porch, and the cock crew   And another maid saw him, and began to say "This is one of them." And he denied again. And a little after, they that stood by said again, "Surely thou art one of them, for thou art a Galilean, and thy speech agreeth thereto." But he began to curse and swear, saying, "I know not this Man of Whom ye speak." The other disciples merely forsook Him. Peter not only forsook, but also denied Him thrice, and with oaths, after having declared, too, that he loved Him more than all the rest. He, beyond all others had fallen, and forfeited his apostleship.

Now come the remarks of Christ, being about to install the Apostles just before He ascended. He turns to St. Peter; "Simon, son of Jonas," ("Simon;" He no longer addresses him by his Apostolic name, Peter; He goes back to his old name;) "Simon, son of Jonas, Lovest thou Me more than these my other disciples?" There are two Greek words meaning to love; φιλέω, signifying to love with the warm personal love of human affection, and ἀγαπάω, signifying to love in the higher, reverential, constant and unvarying sense. Christ looks upon Peter now and says, using the strongest word for love, "Dost thou indeed love Me in the highest sense, and love Me, too, more than all the rest of my disciples?" We can well see Peter hanging his head, and, in view of the recent past, venturing to use not the strongest word but the milder, φιλῶ, and responding simply, "Yea, Lord, Thou knowest that I love Thee with the personal love of human affection." Christ, still bending His mild eye upon him, says "Feed my lambs." And then, after a pause, " Simon, son of Jonas, if thou dost not love Me more than the rest, lovest thou Me in the higher, reverential, constant and unvarying sense?" Christ still insists on the strong word for love, although He drops all allusion to Simon's loving Him more than the others loved Him. St. Peter, scarcely looking up, still using the other word, φιλῶ, responds, "Yea, Lord, Thou knowest that I love Thee." Jesus saith unto him, "Tend my sheep." And, a third time, after a pause, with the same mild eyes fixed upon him, with the same forgiving look, Jesus says, no longer insisting even upon the ἀγαπάω, but coming down to Simon's word, " Simon, son of Jonas, lovest thou Me with warm human affection only?" "Lord," was Simon's reply, " Thou knowest all things ; Thou knowest that I love Thee." " Feed my sheeplings."

O, what a mild and beautiful rebuke for those three cruel denials. How kind, how considerate was our gentle Saviour in furnishing this opportunity for

Peter, chastened by the past, to reinstate himself upon a true basis, and in presence of the rest of the Apostles. Judas had lost his Apostleship entirely. St. Peter had forfeited his three times over, and under most aggravating circumstances. Judas had fallen, and there was danger of Peter also being regarded by the other Apostles as unworthy of even equality with them. But as he had thrice denied the Lord, our Lord thus three times calls him to confess his love for Him before all the Apostles. He thus reinstates him; and then commissions all together.

Rome claims that. in this passage, Christ used the different Greek words, viz., βόσκε, to feed, with regard to the lambs, and ποίμανε, tend, guide, or perform all the duties of a shepherd, with regard to the sheep. And she claims that the lambs mean the laity, and the sheep the clergy, including the Bishops; Feed the former, Rule the latter. But, first, it is gratuitous to claim that the lambs and sheep mean anything more than children and adults. Secondly, It is unfortunate for the supposition that the sheep here means all the Apostles, whom Peter was to rule, that, in the only place in the New Testament where the Apostles are spoken of as sheep at all, St. Peter is included among them; "I send you forth as sheep in the midst of wolves." And it is furthermore unfortunate for Rome, that even if ποίμανε means tend or rule, the passage confers no special privilege on St. Peter; for we have the same word used in the case of even ordinary Priests or elders, far below the Apostles in power and dignity; viz., the Priests of Miletus are commanded by St. Paul to "rule" the Church of God; and St. Peter, using the same word, exhorts the elders "to tend" the flock of God, taking the oversight thereof; the flock; that is to say, the lambs and the sheep. Indeed, some of the early writers have been careful to point out that the privilege thus accorded to St. Peter, was by no means peculiar to him. "Christ Himself," says St. Basil, "gave to all succeeding pastors and teachers a like authority." And St. Augustine says, "In that it was said to St. Peter, it was said to all, ' Feed my sheep.' "

The Second text on which Rome bases her claim is the famous passage, " Thou art Peter, and upon this Rock I will build my Church." Let us see whether the passage will bear out the claim. What were the circumstances in which this remark was made? The Blessed Lord had come; He had chosen His Apostles; He had presented Himself to the people by teaching and by miracles. As man, He was anxious to know whether He was understood. He asks His twelve friends, "Whom do men say that I am." They answered "Some say this, some that." Ah; but how was it with His chosen few? Did they realize His mission, and Who He really was? "But whom say *ye* that I am?" St. Peter, with his usual impetuosity, spoke first; "Thou art the Christ, the Son of the Living God." Now this was precisely what Christ was anxious to elicit from them. This was what He longed to have the people also know and feel. But, first, His twelve must thoroughly realize it. This great fact, that He was the Messias, was clearly the uppermost, the lowermost, the absorbing topic in His mind at the time He was speaking. Is it natural for Him instantly to drop that, and state another thought; or is it natural for Him to carry that same idea along? Peter was the only one of the twelve, so far, that seemed to be thoroughly convinced. He turns quickly to Peter, therefore, and replies, as it were, "Yes; you have spoken rightly; I am the Christ—the God-man; and upon this eternal Rock I will build my Church."

But besides this naturalness in the flow of the thought of the moment, the Blessed Lord positively did not say at all in this passage that He would build

His Church on Peter. The very passage itself says that He would build it on something other than St. Peter. This fact does not appear under our English translation; but it appears unmistakably in the original Greek. For the word translated Peter does not mean a Rock at all. Just as there are two words in English, namely, stone, meaning a pebble, and rock, meaning a great ledge, so there are two corresponding words in Greek. The masculine word δ πέτρος, or Peter, means a stone. The feminine word, ἡ πέτρα, means something else; it means a great rock. Now if the Lord had meant to say He would build His Church on Peter, He would have said so; He would have said " Thou art Peter, o petros, a stone, and upon this petros, this stone, this Peter, I will build my Church " No, but He changed the word to the feminine, petra; " Thou art o petros, a stone, and, not upon this stone, but upon this Petra, this Rock, which thou hast just announced, this Christ the Son of the Living God, will I build my Church."

The only reply of the Romanists to this unanswerable argument, is one that Bellarmine's ingenuity suggested, namely; that our Lord spoke in Syriac and not in Greek; and that, in Syriac, He did not change the word from stone to rock, but used the same word in both clauses, saying, "Thou art Cepha, and upon this Cepha I will build my Church." But there are only five difficulties about this reply.

First. It is guess-work on the part of Bellarmine. For it is not known now whether our Lord spoke at the time in Greek or in Syriac.

Secondly. Even if Bellarmine's unproved assertion were true, we should still be "compelled to accept St. Matthew's variation of the two words, as divinely inspired for the express purpose of marking the difference" between the stone, Peter, and the Rock, Christ.

Thirdly. The Roman Catholic, at any rate, cannot raise this plea at all. He is shut out from it, because he is bound by the decrees of Trent to accept the Latin Vulgate Bible as holy and canonical; and that Version uses two different words, Petrus and Petram; making the same distinction between pebble and Rock that is found in the Greek.

Fourthly. It so happens (although Bellarmine did not chance to know it,) that both the Hebrew and the Syriac word when it means *rock* is feminine; which Cephas, as a masculine noun denoting a man's name, certainly is not.

And lastly. It also happens that, in the Syriac version of the Bible itself, Bellarmine's unproved statement about Cephas is not sustained. For the same difference is found in the Syriac that the Greek presents; for the feminine pronoun is actually united to the second Cepha, and not to the first.

So that Bellarmine's rejoinder breaks down all round and utterly.

Indeed the Apostles are often called, in Scripture, stones, but never a Rock; while Christ Himself is often called a Rock. Besides, "if the Infinite and Almighty God was the Rock of the Elder Israel, while St. Peter, a mere man, was the rock of Christendom, then the Gospel has sunk unspeakably and immeasurably below the Law; which is contrary to all analogy of faith."

"Of all the Fathers who interpret this passage," say the able Roman Catholic divines who wrote Janus, "not one single one applies the words to the Roman Bishops as St. Peter's successors. How many fathers have busied themselves with the text, yet not one of them whose commentaries we have, Origen, Chrysostom, Hilary, Augustine, Cyril, Theodoret, and those whose interpretations are collected in catenas, has dropped the faintest hint that the Primacy of Rome is the consequence of this remark of Christ's. Not one of them has explained the Rock, or foundation on which Christ would build His Church, as being any office given to St. Peter to be transmitted to his successors; but they understood by it either Christ Himself, or St. Peter's confession of faith in Christ; often both together. Or else they thought Peter was the foundation equally with the other Apostles, the twelve being together the foundation stones of the Church."

The Lord is evidently speaking of no subordinate, but of the chief part of the Church's basis. And when we come down to plain simple facts, stripped of all subtleties, if the Church is built on the foundation of the Apostles and Prophets, surely it is no less than Jesus Christ Himself that is the Chief corner-stone, and not St. Peter.

It is very strange, too, if the Lord had by this passage given the Supremacy to St. Peter, that the disciples should not have known it; but should be found, shortly after, discussing as to who was to have precedence in Christ's Kingdom; and that our Lord, instead of reminding them that He had already appointed Peter as their head, should reply in terms inconsistent with that; and that, a little later, He should again put them all on a level; "Ye shall sit upon twelve thrones, judging the twelve tribes of Israel."

When the Lord, after His resurrection, said to St. Peter, "Follow thou Me," and Peter turned and asked, "Lord, and what shall this man do?" "It is obvious that, if St. Peter had received jurisdiction over St. John, his question would have been perfectly legitimate and reasonable, and would have merited a reply as being his concern, because affecting one for whom he had been made responsible. But the answer he received," "What is that to thee?" denotes the restriction of St. Peter's commission to his own share of Apostolic work, with no right of control over St. John.

Besides, both St. Luke and St. Mark, who was St. Peter's amanuensis, omit this text entirely. Hence it is clear that, in their minds, the important part of the conversation was the declaration of our Lord's Person and Office, and not any definition about St. Peter. And it is evident that St. Peter, in supervising St. Mark's gospel, did not himself consider it necessary to communicate this text, on which Rome relies for the Supremacy, to those for whom his Gospel was written; "and, therefore, it is clear that he did not himself attach the meaning to it which Rome claims it has. For, had he done so, he was bound, for the highest reasons, to make his peculiar commission known; precisely as an ambassador is required to produce his credentials at his entry upon his office. Nor can such a breach of duty as silence on his part be excused under such circumstances by attributing it to St. Peter's humility; because the truest humility is implicit obedience to God's commands, whether tending to exalt or abase him to whom the command is given."

If St. Peter had succeeded in any special sense to Christ's authority over the Church as His Vicar, and "if, in consequence, the Apostolic College bore any such relation to him as, for instance, the College of Cardinals does to the Pope—and the Roman theory requires no less—then, certainly, St. Peter would, after the Ascension have filled up the vacant place of Judas on his own authority." But he does nothing of the kind. He merely suggests that the place be filled; but it is the whole College that nominates, and the vacancy is filled by their ballots.

Moreover, when the College of Apostles heard that Samaria had received the Word of God, they sent Peter and John to administer Confirmation. Now "it is a maxim, admitting of no exception in human affairs, that the sender is greater than the sent. And, therefore, the Apostolic Board at Jerusalem was, in its totality, greater than St. Peter." How would a similar transaction seem to us to-day? How would such an announcement as this sound, says a late writer in the " Church Quarterly," to whom I am indebted for some of the above quotations, viz : " The College of Cardinals at Rome, having heard that a dispute as to liturgical questions had arisen at Lyons, sent the Pope and Cardinal Simeoni to settle it?" Why such a thing is inconceivable. And yet the Board of Apostles sent Peter and John.

Furthermore, if Christ had given the Supremacy to St. Peter, surely St. Peter would have presided at the first General Council at Jerusalem, and announced its decision. But, on the other hand, it was St. James that took this precedency.

Besides, how does it happen that the only inspired letters of instruction to Bishops should have been penned by St. Paul and not by St. Peter? How happens it that, as soon as St. Paul appears in the Acts of the Apostles, he completely overshadows St. Peter, and St. Peter almost disappears from mention? How happens it, on the theory that St. Peter was Ruler and sole Doctor of the Church, that St. Paul's writings are not only fourteen times in excess of St. Peter's in mere bulk, but have been incomparably "the most powerful factor in moulding the life and tenets of the Church?"

If the plenitude of teaching and ruling was vested in St. Peter, how happens it that the chief store-house of doctrine and disciplinary instructions is in St. Paul's, St. James's, St. John's writings; anywhere, in fact, instead of St. Peter's? "It is impossible to reconcile these broad facts with the position claimed for the Popes as chief rulers and teachers of the Church in virtue of their heirship to St. Peter."

Then again, St. Paul makes a remarkable statement in this passage, viz.: "When they saw that the Gospel of the uncircumcision was committed unto me, as the Gospel of the circumcision was unto Peter, (for He that wrought effectually in Peter to the apostleship of the circumcision, the Same was mighty in me towards the Gentiles,)" etc. Here, "instead of the Church Universal being, so to speak, St. Peter's diocese, he was, after making the first gentile converts, divinely restricted to the Jewish converts; and had no jurisdiction whatever over the gentiles. How is this consistent with any divine appointment of St. Peter to universal jurisdiction?"

St. Paul, too, claims that "the care of all the churches" came upon him daily. Not a word of the kind from St. Peter. Tenfold more are the texts that would seem to elevate St. Paul, than the three only which diligent search has found to do duty for St. Peter. St. Chrysostom, indeed, styles the Apostle of the Gentiles, " The Apostle of the world," " The planter of the Church," " The foundation of the faith," " The pillar and ground of the truth." If he had said this of St. Peter, our ears would have been dinned with the cry of this quotation.

How does it happen that St. Paul and St. James resisted St. Peter to the face; in a case, too, where it eventuated that St. Peter was wrong? And how happens it that not in one single instance did St. Peter either exercise, or claim to exercise, Supremacy or even Primacy?

St. Augustine says in his Retractions, " I said, in a certain place, of the Apostle Peter, that on him, as on a Rock, the Church is founded. But I am aware that afterwards I very frequently expounded the words as said of our Lord. Peter being so named from the Rock, Petra, and thus representing the Church Which is built upon the Rock. For it was not said to him, 'Thou art the Rock, the Petra,' but 'Thou art Pet*ros*.' The Rock, the Petra, was Christ, Whom Simon confessing, as the whole Church confesses Him, was called Petros." *

* Retractions, I. xxi., A.D. 428.

The Third text which Rome alleges in support of the Pope's claims is, "I will give unto thee (Peter) the Keys of the Kingdom of Heaven." But this text fails as a support quite as utterly as that about the Rock. For our Lord indeed *promised* that He would give Peter the Keys. But, shortly after, He made the self-same *promise*, in the same words, to all the other Apostles. And when, after His Resurrection, He fulfilled these promises touching binding and loosing, He gave the Keys to all the Apostles equally; of course, fulfilling His promise both to St Peter and to the rest. So that the power of the Keys is by no means St. Peter's exclusive right, but was given to the Combined Episcopate as the great Vicar of Christ. In reference to this passage, Origen asks incredulously, "What! are the Keys given by the Lord to Peter only?" St. Ambrose distinctly teaches that "What is said to Peter, is said to the Apostles (as a body)." St. Augustine writes, "These Keys were received not by one man, but by the unity of the Church. Did Peter receive the Keys, and not Paul? Peter, and not John and James and the rest of the Apostles?"*

These three, then, are the passages on which Rome bases her claim that Peter is supreme by divine appointment and right.

* S. Augustine Sermons, ccxcv. 2, SS. Peter and Paul.

We have only examined Scripture. We have not touched the equally strong historical argument at all.

What more miserable attitude for a vast pyramid can be conceived, than for it to be standing balanced on its apex. The vast pyramid of the Papal Supremacy stands upside down and rests on these three Scripture texts. They are the guarantee of its poise and its security. But, if I mistake not, you have seen that its apex is not granite, but melting ice.

SIXTH CONFERENCE.

THE PAPAL AUTOCRACY NOT SUSTAINED BY HISTORY. CONCLUSION.

GENTLEMEN,

We have found Rome's claim to possess the Primacy by Divine right, to be quite unwarranted by Scripture. We have seen that Scripture, on the other hand, is clear in stating that Christ founded the Church on Himself as Its corner-stone, and not on St. Peter; and gave the keys to the whole College of Apostles instead of to St. Peter alone. We have found that St. Peter never exercised, or even claimed a Primacy; which, as a humble man, obedient to God, he was bound to do, had Christ given it to him; that, though he seemed to be prominent among the Apostles at first, as being the man of strongest character among them, and probably the oldest, yet that he is completely overshadowed by St. Paul, as soon as the latter appears on the scene; and, furthermore, that St. Peter's personal jurisdiction, far from being in the end universal, was actually restricted to the

Jewish converts, while St. Paul, as Apostle of the Gentiles, had all the rest of the churches committed to him by the Holy Ghost.

If, then, the Bishop of Rome is found in after time, as is the fact, with a universal Primacy of Honor, such Primacy must have had an ecclesiastical origin subsequent to the times of the Apostles. Leaving Scripture and St. Peter, then, let us come to history. Here also Catholicity rests her position with the utmost confidence.

We search in vain in the writings of the immediate successors of the Apostles, namely, of the Apostolic Fathers, Sts. Clement, Polycarp, Ignatius and Barnabas, for any evidences of a Primacy of any kind in Rome. We search in vain for such evidence through that document of the second century known as the Apostolic Canons. Catholicity asserts, then, that sometime subsequently to the Apostles and the Apostolic Fathers, Our Lord, acting through His Great Vicar the Combined Episcopate, granted a Primacy of Honor to the Bishops of Rome ; and this not because they were successors of St. Peter, but solely because Rome was the capital city of the world. The Bishop of Rome at that time, therefore, united in himself several ecclesiastical dignities. He was

Bishop of his diocese, Archbishop also of his Province, Patriarch of the Patriarchate consisting of Corsica, Sardinia, Sicily, and Italy below the forty-fourth parallel of latitude, and, lastly, so far as the whole Church was concerned, universal Primate of Honor. Catholicity asserts that the Great Vicar of Christ, the Combined Episcopate, did not at that time abdicate, and has never since abdicated its supreme power in General Council, that it has never destroyed itself by giving to the Bishop of Rome a legislative, judicial and executive Primacy over other Patriarchates than his own, still less the Autocracy over the whole church.

Catholicity claims that, by slow degrees, and by the pursuit of a consistent policy of aggression, the Bishops of Rome, starting on this slender foundation of a Primacy of Honor, acquired, through their power, wealth and influence as Prelates of the capital city of the world, function after function in the West, until at last the modern Supremacy is the result. In short, just as in the State, monarchies slowly emerged out of the powerful aristocracies of feudal times, so in the Church the Papal monarchy slowly reared itself in the west over Episcopal power; and as in the State the monarchs gradually became absolute, until we have such Kings as Louis XIVth of France, so in the Church the Papacy also became absolute until we have such Pontiffs as Gregory the Seventh ; and as in the State this absolutism was succeeded by the beheading of Charles First, the Revolution of 1688, the French and American Revolutions, and by anarchy generally, so in the Church the Papal absolutism was followed by the religious revolts and anarchies of the sixteenth and subsequent centuries.

But surely, gentlemen, to-day we have harbinger of better times. Your very call for these conferences is one of the minor but unmistakable notes of the dawn. Surely the constitutional governments which are now succeeding the anarchies in state, are, in God's Providence, preparing men's minds to hate in Religion both the many-headed individualism and chronic anarchy of Protestantism, and the one-headed absolutism of Rome, and to restore that wise constitutionalism in Church also, which God eighteen hundred years ago provided for Catholicity, but which the ambition of Rome invaded. This divine Constitutionalism in Church is the safeguard of the Bishop, the Priest, the Deacon and the laymen.

A quickened action of blood in the arm under exercise is a healthy process. But an increase of blood there amounting to an inflammation is disease; which, unless it is checked, will in the end kill the whole body. Now the difference between the healthy action of the blood and the earliest beginnings of inflammation is faint. And so the difference between Rome's early Primacy of Honor on the one hand, and, on the other, her later Primacy of functions and her subsequent Autocracy was at first very faint. The divergence between them was like the divergence between two straight lines, which start from the same point with barely a shade's difference in their several directions; but follow them along for sixteen hundred miles, and they come out vastly far apart. Rome prefers the diseased limb; Protestantism would slay the whole body; Catholicity would restore the limb to health.

The slight divergence which took place in the fourth and fifth centuries, between ambitious Rome's Primacy of Honor and what has since become her modern Autocracy, was yielded to at the time by many a Bishop, who, had he known what it would long subsequently eventuate in, would have been as firm in resistance to it, as the Eastern Church was from the first, and as Catholicity has been ever since. We today, however, cannot blame those ancient Bishops very much, when we consider that it took England a thousand years to shake off the absolute monarchy that was emerging and establishing itself in the western part of the Church.

Rome's argument with an ill-instructed Churchman to-day is wily. I do not say the Romanist is wily; I speak only of his argument. A sincere man may use a wily argument. So much the more therefore should that ill-instructed Churchman be on his guard. Unfortunately, too, Rome's argument is reinforced by that Churchman's ignorance, or positively false education. Besides, it is proverbial, that a falsehood that is all a falsehood is an easy thing to dispose of, but a falsehood that is partly a truth is always the worst kind of a lie, being a complicated thing to expose. The uninstructed or falsely instructed and prejudiced Churchman, if Rome can once get his ear, is, first, astonished at finding that, as a positive fact, the Bishop of Rome was after all universal Primate in the Early Church. He had never dreamed of such a thing. He now does not know what to think. The armor of his mere prejudice (proved brittle and worthless,) falls from around him and leaves him helpless He grows indignant at his old teachers as blind guides. He loses all confidence in them. With a growing confidence in his new Roman friend he flies to him for further information. The latter, perfectly cool, recognizes, with more or less of secret joy, the advantage he has gained, and cultivates it. He makes further statements with great calmness and with great confidence. The awakened seeker draws, as he goes on, no distinction between a Primacy of Honor, a Primacy of functions and an Autocracy, for he knows no distinction. He does not trace in History the imperceptible passage of the first into the second and of the second into the third. Rome mingles, meantime, the different historical proofs, easily found along the centuries, of Supremacy, of Primatial functions, and of Honor, and lays them indiscriminately before him. Proofs for the later Supremacy reinforce proofs for the earlier Primacy of functions; proofs for the earliest mere Primacy of Honor react upon and reinforce the other two. The consistent centuries really seem to him to speak one favorable voice touching the present Papal claim. And then, with this preparation, the poor startled man's mind, grown more and more helpless from want of minute historical information, is just ready to be run back with the utmost ease into Scripture and on to Rome's confidently stated and plausible, "Thou art Peter," and to find itself at last definitively shipwrecked on the Rock. Rome's false theory, like many things that are of mere human contrivance, has the advantage of being easily understood and grasped by an undisciplined mind; Catholicity's true theory, like most Divine things, has the disadvantage of being complicated and not readily grasped. A system like Rome's, in which one man's will is the law for all others, is a simple system in its workings, and easy to comprehend; a system like Protestantism's, where each man's will is a law for himself, is also easy to comprehend; but a constitutional form of government, with its balances, its intricacies, its checks and counterchecks and its resultant happiness to man, requires time and care for its comprehension by one to whom it is all novel.

Thus it has happened that Protestant and Low-church ignorance and prejudice have been, and are Rome's most powerful friends and allies. From the opening of the nineteenth century Low-churchmanship has been the underlying, prolific and sole cause of perversions to Rome. The gymnastic pirouetting of eventual perverts through a little ritualism beforehand does not alter the broad fact. Your speaker has a list of the clerical perversions to Rome that have occurred in the American Church since 1820

There are one or two cases where the early education of those who perverted could not be traced, and is not known. But with the exception of, perhaps, one other case, in every instance the clergymen who have perverted were reared in Low-church or in Latitudinarian views. The one or two recent American perversions, that have occurred within the last ten years, were no exceptions to this general rule.

Let us look now at history. As the Christian Church came up and took definite shape, let us watch and ascertain what that shape was. First of all, the Apostles derived their authority from the Blessed Lord. "All power," said He, "is given unto Me in heaven and earth; go *ye* therefore." In the commission thus given there is no reference, you will perceive, either to any local restrictions, or to any distinction between the Apostles, as if one had received any power of greater extent than the others; "Go *ye*." Thus Christ constituted the Kingdom of God, which extended throughout the earth, into one great Apostolic Diocese; over which, not one Apostle, but the whole body of the Apostles had spiritual authority given them. So far, then, the government of the Christian Church is Episcopal and not Papal. At this very root of matters the ultimate power is clearly vested in the Combined Episcopate as the Vicar of Christ.

Now though this divine commission was given by our Lord to the whole Board of the Apostolate, it does not appear that He intended the Twelve to keep all together as they exercised their ministry. Whatever subdivisions, therefore, of the Apostolic Diocese, that is to say of the whole Kingdom of God on earth, might be expedient, as one Apostle went to one region, and another to another, the arrangement of their several fields of labor was left to the Apostles themselves, and was not ordained by the Lord before the disappearance of His Natural Body. St. Paul, indeed, uses such language as implies that it was customary for each Apostle to abstain from " building on another's foundation." "As the number of the original Apostles was gradually diminished by death, the jurisdiction of the remainder would naturally expand; until, at last, St. John was left for many years the sole living one of the original Apostles; when all strictly Apostolic power would, of course, be centered in him for the rest of his life." It seems to have been during his sole Apostolate that that local Episcopal system of the Church, which had been begun before, as instance the cases of Sts. Timothy in

Ephesus, Titus in Crete, and Mark in Alexandria, was finally arranged, so as to become the permanent system all over the Church. "And it is doubtless in this sense that Tertullian says, 'The order of Bishops, if traced back to its origin, will rest upon John.'" It is very remarkable he does not say upon St. Peter. That was a subsequent invention. Thus the orderly rules, by which a definite field of labor, a diocese, should be mapped out for each Bishop, grew up during the Apostolic period, and so the temporary Apostolic system of jurisdiction was extended into the permanent Diocesan.

In shaping the Church geographically the Apostles were not obliged on principle to conform to the territorial divisions or provinces of the Roman Empire. But practically they seem to have done so. For they often passed through the principal cities of one province and founded the Church, before entering another; and afterwards they treated the faithful of that province as forming one community. "For instance St. Paul writes to the church at Corinth and to all the faithful of Achaia. He thus unites in his thoughts all the Christians of Achaia, and, at the head of the churches of that province, he places that of Corinth, which was its political capital. He addresses in the same manner another of his letters to the Churches of the Galatians; again uniting in his mind all the communities of that civil province." *

The result of this action was, first, the grouping of the Churches of each Province together; and, secondly, the pre-eminence over his colleagues, or the Archi-episcopal rank, of the Bishop of the capital city of the Province. Besides this, the provincial capital was often the first city in a province in which the Church was founded, and from which the Gospel spread to the other subordinate cities. This, therefore, also threw its Bishop into the rank of the Metropolitan of the whole Province, and centered in him the power of taking order for the appointment and consecration of the suffragan Bishops of his Province. In fact St. Titus was evidently left by St. Paul as Archbishop of Crete, and St. Timothy as Archbishop of Ephesus.

It is quite material to observe, that customs which thus grew up of themselves, so to speak, and were found to be convenient, that the Provincial primacies, for instance, which were thus established, together with the powers centering in the Archbishops, became precedents in newly-worked districts; and that subse-

* Hefele.

quently these habits of order and organization, into which the Church practically and naturally fell, were confirmed formally from time to time by the Combined Episcopate in General Councils assembled. The Provincial system, then, thus begun by the Apostles, with its Archbishops and suffragan Bishops, became, first by the authority of the acts of the Apostles themselves, and secondly by the authority of the decrees of the Combined Episcopate, the fixed governmental policy of the Catholic Church. Thus when we pass away from the Apostolic days, we find that the cities of each Province formed the Dioceses of the Bishops, while the Bishop of the capital city was Archbishop of the Province. As the ultimate power of erecting Primacies lay in the Combined Episcopate, the power of destroying any one, or of altering the eminence among them lay there also. Indeed the Councils of Chalcedon and the Trullane ordained, that " If by royal authority any city be, or should hereafter be, re-established, the order of the churches shall be according to the civil form."

Such being the state of things, then, in this Second or Provincial Period of the Church, it is very clear that one result would naturally follow, namely : the mind of the Church would very early have planted within it what we may call "The leading-city idea." Under the influence of this idea there was very early conceded by all, and without opposition, a general Primacy of Honor and of respect to the Bishop of that city which was the great capital city of the world. This was not at first conceded to the Bishop of Rome formally, nor by decree, but by habit of mind. And it was the more readily conceded, since it involved no right of interference on his part with Dioceses or Provinces beyond his own Provincial, or subsequently Patriarchal, jurisdiction. Afterwards this generally conceded fact received the seal of confirmation by the Collective Episcopate in the Second General Council.

But when the Bishop of Rome began to arrogate to himself, on this slender foundation, powers of interference in the East, in England, and in Africa, he was instantly resisted ; and, as he continued, without authorization from General Council, to claim greater and wider powers, the whole Church rocked at last as on an earthquake, and broke into the two Communions, Greek and Latin ; the Greek at the time being the larger of the two. This is standing evidence of the uncatholic nature of the claim of Papal supremacy. But I am anticipating.

All through this Second, or Provincial Period, the Provincial Councils of the Church and the Apostolic Canons do not speak of any offices higher than those of Bishops and Archbishops. But now comes a change in the geographical constitution of the Empire; a corresponding change, therefore, followed in the constitution of the Church. The civil provinces of the Empire were clustered together into groups, and a leading city was erected for each group. Let me take an illustration, which, though not exactly parallel, will serve our purpose. Suppose, for instance, we should cluster the New England States together into one political group; and erect over the separate State governors an Arch-governor for the whole group; and the Middle States into another group; and the Southern into another, and so on. This will give you to understand the new organization of the Roman Empire at the period we are now considering. By the time the Nicene Council meets, in the year 325, we find that the Church is accommodating Herself to this new state of things; and the Combined Episcopate, in that Council assembled, recognizes and confirms the order which it finds. The Bishop of the leading city of each group of provinces was subsequently called Patriarch or Exarch.

This name of Patriarch does not, indeed, appear yet in conciliar canons; but nevertheless the Patriarchal powers which had already centered, for instance, in the Bishops of Rome, Alexandria and Antioch, are recognized by the Fathers of the Nicene Council, and confirmed in their possessors by the Combined Episcopate. Not one word, however, not one hint is dropped that the Bishop of Rome has any jurisdictional powers over the whole Church. The solitary reference to his powers made by the Fathers of Nice is in their sixth canon. But this canon only speaks of his Patriarchal powers. It ordains that, as the Bishop of Rome possesses authority over his Patriarchate, (consisting, as has been said above, of the provinces of Central and Southern Italy with the adjacent islands,) so the Bishop of Alexandria should have like powers over the provinces of Egypt, Libya and Pentapolis; and it confers similar Patriarchal powers on the Bishop of Antioch. According to these powers, appeals could now go up in each Patriarchate beyond the Archbishops of Provinces and to the Patriarch of the group of Provinces; and the latter could, furthermore, take order for the selection and consecration of the Archbishops beneath him, as the Archbishops could still take order for the consecration, each of his own suffragan Bishops.

Then in the Second General Council, which met in the year 381, we have this Patriarchal Period more distinctly emphasised; for we have powers similar to those held by Rome, Alexandria and Antioch, recognized by the Combined Episcopate as having rightly come to reside also in the great Bishops of Ephesus, Cesarea, and Constantinople; and those powers are formally confirmed to them.

But still in the decrees of this Council we search in vain for the recognition or confirmation by the Episcopate of any general powers, executive, legislative or judicial, over the whole Church as residing in the Bishop of Rome. We simply find that his Primacy of Honor, and nothing more, is acknowledged, and, for the first time, confirmed. This was in the year 381.

The reference which the Council makes to the matter is in its third canon. The Bishop of Constantinople had previously stood sixth in rank among the six great Bishops. Owing to the fact, however, that the capital of the Empire had recently been changed from Rome to Constantinople, the Council now alters his rank from the sixth up to the second place. The canon reads; "The Bishop of Constantinople shall have the Primacy of Honor after the Bishop of Rome, because that now Constantinople is new Rome." The Primacy of Honor: not a word about universal Supremacy. If we count the Apostolic times as the First Period of the Church, and the Provincial as the Second Period, we have reached here the Third or Patriarchal Period. The Dioceses are grouped into Provinces, with an Archbishop over each. The Provinces are grouped, except those in the far west of Europe, England among them, and except a few in the East, which are still left autocephalous, into Patriarchates with a Patriarch over each. The Head of the whole Church, the vicar of Christ, is the Collective Episcopate, speaking and acting in General Council. Finally within the Episcopate, but not over it, are two leading Primacies of Honor; first, the Bishop of Old Rome, and next to him the Bishop of New Rome.

By the time the Fourth General Council met, that namely of Chalcedon, a century and a half subsequently, we have not only the office but also the name itself of Patriarch or Exarch mentioned in the Conciliar decrees. Still no erecting of the Bishop of Rome into the position of Autocrat; but only a firmer recognition still of the self-same post of honor, without any addition, which the Episcopate in its previous Councils had confirmed. For the XXVIIIth canon of this Fourth General Council, which is the only one having a bearing on the subject, reads: " We, following in all things the decisions " of the second General Council, "do *also* determine and decree the same things respecting the privileges of the most holy city of Constantinople, New Rome. For the Fathers properly gave the Primacy" (and by reference to the Second Council we find that Primacy was distinctly stated in Canon III to be a Primacy of Honor)—" the Fathers properly gave the Primacy to the throne of the Elder Rome, because that was the imperial city. And, being moved with the same intention, they gave equal privileges to the most holy Throne of New Rome ; judging, with reason, that the city which was honored with the sovereignty and senate, and which enjoyed equal privileges with the Elder royal Rome, should also be magnified like her in ecclesiastical matters, being the second after her." Thus the Combined Episcopate in 451 confirmed and explained what it had previously done in the year 381.

Indeed whatever may be said touching Chalcedon's

famous twenty-eighth canon, Catholicity needs only this canon in combination with the third of the Second General Council, and nothing more, to prove beyond dispute her position, that the Combined Episcopate was, according to the Apostolic Constitution of the Church, the Great Vicar of Christ, in which all ultimate power rested ; that it created Primacies and Patriarchs within itself; that it changed them, and their order of precedence, at will ; and that it gave even his general Primacy of Honor to the Bishop of Rome. For mark how the canon reads; "The *Fathers*"—not Christ—"properly *gave* the Primacy of Honor to the Throne of the Elder Rome, because" —why? Because it was Rome's by divine right? No. Because it was St. Peter's throne? No. Because Christ said, "Thou art Peter," and "Feed my sheep?" No. But solely, "*because that was the imperial city.*" And the Fathers of the second General Council, the Combined Episcopate, *gave* equal privileges to the Patriarch of Constantinople, because that had become the New Rome. What more do we need? We could close our case just here with confidence. But let us proceed with history. Indeed the order of rank among the Bishops of the leading cities was changed by the Combined Episcopate from time to time according to circumstances. At first the chief see was Jerusalem, and some authors give the sequence thus: "Jerusalem, Cæsarea, Antioch, Rome, Alexandria." But however this may have been, we come, at any rate, to a time when the order was certainly this, namely: " Rome, Alexandria, Antioch, Cæsarea and Constantinople." And then afterwards came a time when the order was changed by the Episcopate into " Rome, Constantinople, Alexandria, Antioch, Ephesus, Cæsarea, and Jerusalem."

To return; we have reached a time, in the Third or Patriarchal Period, when the Bishops of the few leading cities of the world were getting up upon thrones; and Rome in the West, and Constantinople in the East on the highest thrones of all. The natural effect of this was to reinforce the arrogance and ambition of Rome. But it also providentially increased the power of Constantinople to resist Rome, in the interest of the ancient Episcopal Constitution of the Church, which Rome was already striving to change, first into a monarchial form of government, and then into an absolute Autocracy. The whole East with Constantinople, together with Africa, steadily resisted these growing claims of Rome. Meantime Mahomet swept through Africa and wiped out the noble churches of Carthage. The collisions increased between Constantinople on the one hand, and Rome on the other. These struggles could not have occurred, had such a thing been understood from the first by the Church as that Supremacy had been centered in Rome originally and by "divine right." Meantime Rome was growing yearly stronger in the unorganized far west, invading, with little or with ineffectual resistance, the outlying Churches of Spain, Gaul and Britain, which had not been clustered into an organic Patriarchate, and which looked with respect, therefore, and, with the exception of England, with more and more willing submission, to their powerful neighbor the Patriarch of Italy.

But at last, as I have said, the collision between Rome and the East eventuated in the great rupture of the ninth century. The four Eastern Patriarchates on the one hand, and the one Western Patriarchate of Rome on the other, ceased intercommunion with each other, and we have the Fourth Period of the Church begun, in which the west, the barbarous part, that is to say, is freed by excommunication from the East or more enlightened part, and the East is freed from the overbearing ambition and attempted Papal encroachments of the West; each of the two carrying off into isolation from the other its part of the Apostolic Ministry, and continuing Its succession and Its consequent Sacraments down to to-day.

During this Fourth Period, the Patriarch of Rome, thus left free and unrestrained, grew more and more supreme and autocratic in the West, until a similar rupture occurred in the Western part of the Church, whereby it separated into the Anglican and Latin Communions; and the Fifth Period opened; each Communion, Roman and Anglican, carrying off its part of the Apostolic ministry, and continuing its succession down to to-day.

Meantime, during this Fifth Period, the Bishop of Rome developed his Supremacy logically into Infallibility; when the strain again became too great, and another rupture took place; Rome dividing now into New, or Roman Catholics and Alt or old Catholics. This rupture opens the Sixth or present Period of Catholicity. In this period we have the division of the whole Church into two main parts, viz: Catholic and Roman Catholic; the Greek, Anglican, and Alt-Catholics being substantially one in their firm stand for the ancient Episcopal government of the Catholic Church, in opposition to the modern autocratic Papal government, which is a pure absolute monarchy.

Thus we find that down to the middle of the fifth century, when the Fourth General Council met, the Combined Episcopate still retained to itself, and never abdicated in favor of Rome, the ultimate power and the Supremacy over the Church. Indeed to have done so would have been to commit the crime of self-murder, which is the last thing we are to expect of it in our historical research. And this is an unanswerable *à priori* argument that it is quite impossible for Rome ever to have acquired the Supremacy of the whole Catholic Church. She can only have a Supremacy in her own part of the Church, indeed, by the destruction of the rights of her Bishops. And this is just what she has at last succeeded in doing. For let me read to you the noble words of the Archbishop of Halifax, uttered at the recent Vatican Council of 1870. In that Council the entire body of Roman Bishops, having been for centuries laboring in the trough of the sea, foundered at last and sank finally in the tempestuous waves of Papal power. And the words of Archbishop Conolly are like the wail of shipwrecked mariners when all hope is gone. He spoke as follows:

"Thrice have I asked for proof from Scripture according to authentic interpretation, from tradition, and from Councils, that the Bishops of the Catholic

Church ought to be excluded from the definition of dogmas; but my request has not been complied with. And now I adjure you, like the blind man on the way to Jericho, to give us sight, that we may believe. Hitherto we have recognized the strongest motive for the credibility of Catholic doctrine in the general consent of the Church, notified through the Collective Episcopate. This has been our shield against all external assailants; and by this powerful magnet we have drawn hundreds of thousands into the Church. Is this, our invincible weapon of attack and defence, now to be broken and trampled under foot; and the thousand-headed Episcopate, with the millions of faithful at its back, to shrink into the voice and witness of a single man? Let the deputation prove to us that it has really always been the belief of the Church that the Pope is everything and the Bishops nothing. The Council of Jerusalem did not adopt the formula of Peter, but of John who spake before him; and in the Apostles' Creed we do not say, 'I believe in Peter and his successors,' but, 'I believe in one Catholic Church.' We, Bishops, have no right to renounce for ourselves and our successors the hereditary and original rights of the Episcopate; to renounce the promise of Christ, 'I am with *you* to the end of the world.' But now they want to reduce us to nullities; to tear the noblest jewel from our pontifical breast-plate; to deprive us of the highest prerogative of our office; and to transform the whole Church, and the Bishops with It, into a rabble of blind men, among whom is one alone who sees; so that they must shut their eyes and believe whatever he tells them."

Indeed the attitude of the minority, of nearly two hundred out of six hundred Bishops, in that Vatican Council was pitiable. They made brave struggle to retain the remnant of the Episcopal rights which previous Papal usurpations had left them; but it was a struggle against invincible logic. For, their predecessors had sowed the wind, and what could they expect but to reap the whirlwind? For, the Roman Episcopate, having previously given up the Primacy of Honor and accepted the Papal Supremacy instead, had already erected a power among themselves, before which they were compelled at last to stand helpless, as it easily snatched from their hands the poor remaining fragments of their rights.

Now as we find no Papal Supremacy authorized down to the year 451, so too we look in vain through the acts of the Fifth and Sixth General Councils for any abdication on the part of the Collective Episcopate of the Vicariate of Christ in favor of the Bishop of Rome. And this brings us to the year 680. The collisions were now such between Rome and the whole body of the eastern Bishops, and the final rupture between the two was so impending on this very question of the Papal Supremacy, that it is clear no action was taken then, or has ever since been taken by the Collective Episcopate of the whole Church, to relinquish its position of Vicar, and resign in favor of the single Bishop of Rome. The only action has been the breaking away of the Anglican and Alt-Catholics from the Papal position, and the adding of their forces as reinforcements to the Eastern Catholic position.

May it not be that, as the See of Rome, with a fatal logical momentum, develops doctrine after doctrine and practice after practice, (for how, foi instance, can she stop short of Pope-olatry?) national Church after national Church, finding the strain becoming too severe, will follow the great example of England, break away from Rome, and pass over to the side of the Catholic Communions, until at last little or nothing is left to adore the Pope; and that so God will at once, in His own deliberate way, eventually purge Catholicity of Popery, "restore communion between the divided members of the Catholic Church, in the East and in the West," and, thus overruling men's errors, cause His Church to stand once more a unit of the highest order, a unit differentiated within itself into variety and complexity? We know not what is in God's purposes. But, to all human ken, it would seem to be as reasonable to anticipate that the Mississippi would pause and return to its source, as that Rome will not go on with gathering momentum till she develops something which neither God nor man can endure.

Let us now look at the Papal Supremacy from another angle. It certainly belongs to Supremacy to summon General Councils. Did the Pope possess or exercise this power in the early Church? It belongs, and always has belonged to the Bishop to summon a Diocesan Council; to the Archbishop to summon a Provincial, and to the Patriarch to summon a National or Patriarchal Council. If the Pope had analogous jurisdictional powers over the whole Church, to those which Archbishops have over their Provinces, surely he would have summoned the General Councils. But the first General Councils were not summoned by him. And this is proof positive that he had only a

Primacy of Honor; that he did not stand to the whole Church as an Archbishop does to his Province, and that the Head Primacy within the Episcopate was different in kind from the subordinate jurisdictional Primacies. The Bishop of Rome did not summon the First Council in 325; the Second, in 381, was actually celebrated against his will; he did not summon the Third in 431; nor the Fourth in 451; nor the Fifth in 533; this also was celebrated against his wishes; nor did he summon the Sixth in 680. There was another Council, sometimes called the Seventh. It met in the latter part of the eighth century. The Popes did not even summon that. Nor were the Popes even consulted about the summoning of these great Councils. In fact there were times when they even desired a General Council but did not succeed in obtaining one; as Innocent, in the matter of St. Chrysostom, and as Leo learned by experience. Thus the claim to Papal Supremacy breaks down in this direction. It was not until the Pope was free from the whole Eastern part of the Church in the ninth century, that we find him exercising this sovereign power of convoking Councils.

Again, it surely belongs to Supremacy to preside at General Councils. But, beginning with the Coun cil of Jersualem in the year 50, St. James, and not St. Peter, was its President. The Bishop of Rome did not preside at the Nicene Council either in person or by deputy, nor, indeed, did he have any considerable influence or sway there, even though he was Bishop of the capital city of the world. The council of Sardica was in design a General Council, but in effect did not prove so. In that synod the Bishop of Rome did not preside. Nay in its epistle the name of Hosius of Corduba is mentioned even before the name of Julius of Rome. Nor did the Bishop of Rome preside at the Second General Council. He was not present at it either personally or by legates. At the Third, it was St. Cyril of Jerusalem that presided. At the Fourth, it was the Emperor Marcian and his commissaries that presided, though they did not of course vote. At the Fifth, the Patriarch of Constantinople presided, and the Patriarch of Rome was not present even by deputy. At the Sixth Council, in 680, the emperor Constantine IVth presided. In fact, as we look at history, so little was such a thing as the Papal Supremacy dreamed of, that the presidency of these great Councils either fell out according to the Emperor's wishes, or was settled by the election of the Fathers present, or on a tacit regard to some personal eminence in comparison to others present.

Again it would belong to Supremacy to give life and validity, by its approval, to the canons and decrees of General Councils. But, beginning with the Council of Jerusalem, Rome should note that it was not St. Peter who gave formal confirmation to and promulgated its decisions; but it was St. James. And then as for the other Councils, a recent Roman Catholic writer, and a Bishop at that, proves that General Councils have promulgated their dogmatic acts without awaiting the Papal sanction; and not only promulgated them, but put them into execution.

The Council of Nice did not await the approval of St. Sylvester to condemn the Arian Bishops. In the Second General Council, Theodosius the Great gave out immediately the constitution relating to the Macedonian heretics. The same thing took place at Ephesus and Chalcedon (the Third and Fourth General Councils). Long before the Holy see's ratification of the dogmatic decrees became known, the penalties for its violation had been executed. Clearly then, by ancient right, the ultimate authority in the Church rests in the Collective Episcopate, and not in the Bishop of Rome; they, not the Pope, being the Vicar of Christ.

But the Romanist will say to you, why, then, were the canons of Councils sent to the Pope for his confirmation, if the sanction of the see of Rome was not necessary to their validity? But the answer is, that it was customary for canons of General Councils to be sent to all the Bishops; and of course to so eminent a Bishop, also, as was always the Bishop of Rome. Nevertheless, somehow, the canons of the Second General Council were not transmitted to Rome even for its information. As for the Fifth General Council, it actually anathematized Pope Vigilius. Besides, touching this entire subject of the confirmation of the Decrees of General Councils, a very limited knowledge of ecclesiastical history will convince one, that equals confirm the decrees of equals, and often inferiors confirm the decrees of their superiors. The Faith and the decrees of Nice were confirmed not only by the General Councils of Constantinople, Ephesus and Chalcedon, but also by particular councils, such as those of Sardica and Jerusalem. In the collection of letters written after the Council of Chalcedon to the Emperor by the Bishops, whom he had consulted on the authority of this Council, we find many times this formula, or similar ones, viz: "We consent to the decrees of the Holy Fathers, which we confirm by our Faith and our confession." Decrees of the Bishop of Rome have been also confirmed by particular councils. It is quite impossible to see in any confirmations of the decrees of any councils, even by the Bishops of Rome, in the first nine centuries, acts of superior authority. All these confirmations were expressions of that reception which was generally accorded by all portions of the Church to the acts of all really General Councils. Surely the decretal of Pope Vigilius, by which he adhered to the Fifth General Council, was far from being an act of absolute superiority. On the other hand it carries with it the seal of deference and of submission.

Again, the powers of Supremacy are three-fold; legislative, judicial and administrative. The Bishop of Rome claims to-day the first; namely, that his will, expressed by precept, decree or proclamation, shall be law. How was it anciently?

Before the Nicene Council in 325, the Church had no other laws than the divine laws, together with those which each church enacted for itself in Provincial synod, and those which were propagated from one to another by imitation or compliance. Hence several churches varied in points of order and discipline according to local circumstances. No one Bishop then could impose his laws upon another territory than his own. When, once, the Bishop of Rome attempted to induce several churches of Asia-Minor to keep Easter on the same day on which it was kept in the West, he not only met with stout resistance but with sharp rebuke. This whole Easter difficulty, indeed, which was a serious one in early times, was not settled by the Bishops of Rome at all. Not until a General Council legislated on it did the entire Church acquiesce in one rule. To show the condition of things at that time, let me quote from St. Cyprian. He says, " For none of us makes himself a Bishop of Bishops, or by tyrannical terror compels his colleagues to a necessity of obedience; since every Bishop, according to the license of his liberty and power, hath his own freedom, and can no more be judged by another, than he himself can judge another." Can we for a moment conceive of a Roman Bishop to-day writing thus? Would not the Bishop of Rome, if such letter reached him to-day, give very prompt evidence to its writer, that, however it may have been in earlier centuries, one Bishop could, in the nineteenth century at any rate, be judged most effectually, and most practically, too, so far as any farther exercise of his Episcopal authority was concerned, by another?

Secondly; the Pope claims the right of appellate jurisdiction; that all causes of weight be referred to him. How was it with this in the fourth century? The fifth canon of Nice provides that causes may be appealed from Dioceses up to the Provincial synods; but not a word about appeals to the Bishop of Rome. If he had such judicial power from the beginning, as there were so many occasions during those early centuries for exercising such power, there would have been extant in history many clear instances of it. But this is not the case. Rome has done the best she could with this argument. Out of a multitude of cases, she has whipped up two or three cases only, and these quite impertinent to the issue. When the Patriarch of Antioch claimed certain rights over the churches of Cyprus, Innocent, the Roman Patriarch, sustained him in his pretentions. But the Council of Ephesus judged otherwise, and prevailed. Where, then, was the Pope's universal and immediate jurisdiction in the year 431? When, subsequently, the Popes set up this claim of appellate jurisdiction, divers synods, some great, some smaller, protested against, and passed acts contrary to it. So we see resistance to the growing claims of the Pope on every hand. In the middle of the fourth century a Council (not however a General Council) met at a place called Sardica. It passed a decree that, under certain circumstances, Julius, Bishop of Rome, should, as a *personal privilege*, appoint judges to hear the cause of a Bishop on the spot, and in the second instance; with the right to send legates representing himself. This power was not granted to the Bishops of Rome, but to Julius personally. On the strength of this (albeit it was not a decree of any General Council) subsequent Popes attempted to set up their claim of appellate jurisdiction. But it was never recognized by the Eastern or by the African Church. Indeed the African Bishops in 419 wrote to Boniface 1st. "We are resolved not to admit this arrogant claim."

In the code of the Fourth General Council, in the middle of the Fifth century, there is no mention whatever of the see of Rome as an ultimate court of appeal, though its Primacy is implied throughout. "Hence when the subject of its appellate jurisdiction came before the heads of the African Church, among whom was St. Augustine, their deliberate finding, which they reported to the Bishop of Rome, and on which they acted themselves, was as follows; That the Nicene decrees plainly committed both the inferior clergy and the Bishops themselves to their own Metropolitans ; ' having most wisely and justly provided that all things should be determined in the very places where they arise ; * * * especially when every man has liberty, if he be offended with the decision of his judges, to appeal to a Provincial Council, or, if need be,' where? to the Pope ? No ; but ' to a General Council.' "

. Nor did Rome exercise the third right of Supremacy, namely, general administrative power during those ages. In fact a general and wide spread administration of the affairs of the universe from Rome was a sheer impossibility. For it could not take place without a certain machinery and system, clerical officials and the like. But nothing of this kind was dreamt of in Rome during those centuries. "The Bishops of Rome," says the author of Janus, " could exclude neither individuals nor churches from the communion of the Church Universal. They could withdraw their own Church from communion with particular Bishops or Churches, and they often did so ; but this in no wise affected the relations of those Bishops or Churches with other Bishops or Churches. And, on the other hand, if Rome admitted into its Communion one excommunicated by other Churches this did not bring that one into Communion with any other Church."

In the Third century Firmilian uses the following language to Pope Stephen: "How mighty a sin hast thou heaped to thyself in cutting thyself off from so many flocks! For do not deceive thyself; it is thou who hast cut off thine own self; he is the real schismatic, who makes himself an apostate from the communion of the Church's unity."

There are several points which a Roman Catholic will urge on the attention of an ill-instructed Churchman calculated to confound him. I can only find time to instance one now. He will cite cases where the Bishop of Rome went beyond the bounds of his Patriarchate to interfere in the ordination of Bishops. And he will say, Does not this show that the Pope had powers of supremacy co-extensive with the Church? But be not hasty. For, a more careful knowledge of facts shows, that other leading Bishops did the self-same thing. His argument does not sustain his claim therefore; for no one ever thought, because of the same action on the part of other great Bishops, to pretend therefore that *they* ever held universal control. Indeed it not seldom happened, that the Bishop of Rome, and the other great Bishops (who, by the way, were all of them then called "Popes") were checked on such occasions, and that their emissaries were dismissed with disgrace, for interfering with a jurisdiction beyond their bounds. Such was the case with the Bishop of Antioch, when he attempted to interfere in Cyprus. And what is more than all, and decisive of the Pope of Rome's case, the second canon of the Second General Council positively checked and regulated such irregularity, by enacting in reference to the matter, that no one of the great Patriarchs go beyond his Patriarchate and enter upon churches without his borders "for the purpose of ordaining, or exercising *any other ecclesiastical functions*," thus bringing confusion into those Churches. The fact is, certain ecclesiastical customs were growing. Power is apt to accumulate at centers. Patriarchs were invading Provinces that did not belong to them. And the object of this canon was to check this special growth; to recognize it, indeed, as far as it had gone, but to stop it just there, and fix the Church for the future in the condition in which It then was; the Patriarchs to have no further powers. This left certain Provinces, and among them Cyprus and England, under no Patriarch, but autonomic and autocephalous. Now this canon has never been repealed, and is binding to-day on the Bishop of Rome, and on the whole Church. It is standing evidence against the claims of the Roman Patriarch to universal power. It is standing evidence that Rome has altered, at least in the Latin part of the Church, the Constitution of the Catholic Church. Two hundred years afterward, in the year six hundred, Rome entered upon the domain of the British Church, which from the first had lain outside her Patriarchate, and had governed itself. And this canon is standing evidence that, from A. D. 596 to A. D. 1539, the Bishop of Rome was an intruder into and a usurper of powers in the English part of the Church, contrary to the will of a General Council. It is, indeed, even a mistake to suppose that the Saxon part of England was very much indebted to St. Augustine for its conversion to Christianity. For, everywhere else except in Kent it was the clergy in the ancient British and Scottish succession that effected that conversion. And the canon is standing evidence that, to-day, the Romish church in England is a schismatical body.

I need not say to you, gentlemen, that the two topics, which I have had the honor of discussing before you, by no means exhaust the important differences between Catholicity and Romanism. But I am sure you did not expect of me, in three Conferences, that which others have only been able to compass in volumes. And this is my consolation as I bid you farewell, and reluctantly retire from an unfinished work. Enough, however, I trust, has been said to satisfy you that a surrender to Rome is treason to Catholicity.

I cannot, however, pass finally from this rostrum, without giving one most important caution concerning controversial books on the Roman side. In the first place "Latin translations of Greek Fathers, unless they are carefully compared with the Greek originals, can have little dependence placed on them; as they frequently bear the unmistakable stamp of Western prejudice." The interpolations into the text of the Fathers, the alterations of that text, and the downright forgeries of the past are, as a fact, so numerous, so extensive, and so vital, that it requires years of careful study on all sides, and long periods of suspended judgment as to alleged proofs, and the sifting of many books antagonistic to each other, before one who is not a profound historian, or a critical Grecian or Latinist, can come to any really intelligent conclusion. There had been many interpolations and forgeries in the interest of the Roman see before the ninth century But in the year eight hundred and forty-five, when criticism and general intelligence in the west were at their lowest ebb, there appeared what is now known as the Isidorian or False Decretals. For two hundred years the enormity and clumsiness of those bold forgeries have been exposed, and universally admitted. Yet those Decretals were received as genuine for seven long centuries. Marvelously enough, although the present Papal power was mainly built up by and through them, it stands to-day as a permanent edifice, long after the miserable framework, the girders and beams of the Forged Decretals, on which much of it rested, had fallen from within it and been burned up as useless rubbish amid universal jeers. But not only does the structure of the Papal power remain, after that which sustained it has disappeared; but something else remains. For those Decretals, so thoroughly trusted, in their day, and the interpolations in the writings of the Fathers were used by earnest and sincere men, like St. Anselm, for quotations and proofs in favor of Romanism. Later writers just as sincerely quoted these proofs, not from the originals, but from St. Anselm, Gratian and others. And, as proof-quotations, they became stock-in-trade for still later writers, equally sincere. So that, to-day, the fragments of whole centuries of fraud, mistaken zeal and pious credulousness, mingled with better material, lie marvelously confused in the strata of controversy. This complicates matters inexpressibly. Then again, on the other side, there is a vast amount of Protestant misrepresentation afloat concerning Roman Catholicism, which further complicates matters. Now to anyone who knows all these facts, to anyone who has, mayhap, studied the question between Rome and Catholicity, more or less for twenty-five or thirty years, who has been often puzzled and astonished at false statements on both sides, oftener still disgusted at the confusion, occasionally almost ready to give up the question in despair, to such an one, I say, the sight of young men and women, and of the middle-aged, devoting the mere spare time of a few weeks or months to the reading of two or three popular controversial works, that are placed in their hands by Roman Catholic propagandists, and then leaping to a conclusion on the whole complicated matter, rushing over to Rome, turning instantly, and, with new born zeal, hurling back hot-shots at the Anglican Mother that bore them, and Whom they never understood or appreciated in Her true Catholicity when they were with Her, is saddening indeed, not to say pitiable and contemptible.

There is another thing I cannot refrain from saying. It has been admirably put by the English "Church Review." I have not its language, but I remember its idea. It is this. The *theory* of the Anglican Church is thoroughly Catholic. But, owing to Continental raids made upon Her prior to and subsequently to the times of Cromwell, the *practice* of Her Priests and people happens temporarily to be left to-day, in too many ways, un-Catholic. Her Catholic theory will inevitably bring the practice of Her Priests and people out right in the end. It is steadily, and as rapidly as we could expect, doing so now. Let us not toss our shoulder and curl our lip impatiently, like so many flippant boarding-school misses, because our un-Catholic practices are so slow in disappearing. On the other hand the *theory* of Romanism on many fundamental points is thoroughly un-Catholic, and *hopelessly* so; while Rome's *practice*, it is true, still continues in many respects to be Catholic. Now a calm and sensible mind, at any rate, will find far less intellectual difficulty in putting up, for a while, with deficient *practice* in a Body Whose theory is wholly Catholic, than in accepting fundamentally false and uncatholic theories for the sake of some perfection in practice or ritual.

Although Christ did not give the Primacy to St. Peter, yet of course He knew that St. Peter's successors in Rome would, in after time, receive the Primacy through ecclesiastical regulation, and because Rome was the capital of the world. Looking, therefore, on one occasion upon St. Peter, He solemnly said to him " Simon, behold, Satan hath desired to have you that he may sift you as wheat; but I have prayed for thee that thy faith fail not. And when thou art converted, strengthen thy brethren." And yet Rome amuses Herself, after this, with the idea that he, who was once Primate, has been all along invulnerable. By this, our Lord's solemn prophecy, Rome, then, was sooner or later to fall into such plight as to need to turn from her errors; "when thou art converted." But meantime, also, while she was in her false position, the brethren, it seems, were to be weak all around. Is it not indeed so to-day? Rome herself is by no means the happy family she has the shrewdness to appear to the world to be. And is it not true, that all the religious divisions and weaknesses within the whole Catholic Church, and without Its borders too, can be traced back for their source to the ambition and errors of Rome? Ah, gentlemen, but when Rome is converted, then indeed shall you see, as the Lord said, the brethren strengthened all around, and Christianity marching as one organized and invincible Catholic Body against Scepticism, the world and Satan.

Again, Rome is apt to take certain remarks to St. Peter, and apply them unwarrantably to herself. Very well, then, why is she so apt to forget others? She forgets that solemn prophecy, "Thou shalt deny Me thrice;" and that her Peter of the centuries must sooner or later, in an agony of repentance, "go out" and weep bitterly. Hath Rome denied Christ once? She hath, at any rate, struck down His Royal, visible Body, the Episcopate, saying, "Away with you;" and substituted her Pope as Ruler of the Church in Its stead. Hath she denied Christ twice? She hath, at any rate, struck down His Body the Church as the Organ to us of the truth, with curses and anathemas, too, saying "Away with you," "I am the truth." Hath she denied Him thrice? She hath, at any rate, reared between Him and us a mediatrix, as though He, the loving Brother, That died for us, needs to be appeased before we can steal to Him and lie directly upon His bosom.

She has forgotten that prophecy in action, too, namely; St. Paul resisting St. Peter, when he was wrong, to the face. One does not desire to be fanciful. But one cannot help thinking of the great feud to-day as a possible fulfilment of that prophecy; namely, the feud between the mighty Anglican Communion said to be founded by St. Paul, and whose greatest temple is the Cathedral of London, and the vast Communion said to be founded by St. Peter, whose greatest temple is the Cathedral of Rome.

One more word and I have done. The Catholic Church is Christ's Body. And Satan's warfare on the Human part of the God-man did not cease at Calvary. As Satan nailed Him to the Cross, so he follows Him with mighty smitings through the centuries. And Rome's fond idea, that Christ's Body is something that cannot possibly show such ghastly wounds as non-intercommunion between Its parts, or such bruises anywhere as a fundamental local alteration in Its governmental structure, is but a utopian dream; it is to forget the swollen back, the bones stretched out of joint, the nails, the thorns and the spear.

But, meantime, it is a consolation to know, that God is, nevertheless, so overruling the ambition of the See of Rome and its effects in having produced the

Greek, Russo-Greek, Anglican, Alt-Catholic and other Communions, as to differentiate His great Catholic Church, and develop It from the imperfect unity of simplicity into the perfect unity of multiplexity and harmonious variety.

SERMON.

THE OBJECT AND MEANING OF THE CATHOLIC MOVEMENT
IN THE ANGLICAN COMMUNION.

Preached at Zion Church, Newport, R. I., at the request of the Rector of that Church.

IMMANUEL.—ISA. vii. 14.

NEARLY half a century ago a remarkable fraternity of young men arose in Oxford. Perceiving that the Prayer Book taught the doctrines which were set forth by the Early Church, but that Churchmen generally in 1833 did not hold them, these young men issued the "Tracts for the Times," with the design of arousing the minds of Churchmen, and bringing them into agreement with the statements of the Prayer Book and the teachings of the Early Church. Thus was inaugurated the great Catholic movement in the Anglican Communion.

To a non-Churchman, unfamiliar with the career of the English Church from 1620 to 1833, the statement that She should teach one thing, and Her members believe another, would seem not only paradoxical but incredible. But, without delaying this discourse by entering upon History, let it be remembered that when Cromwell assumed the reins of power, he crushed the Church of England; he drove Her clergy from their livings; and for years the people of England were indoctrinated by Presbyterian, Independent and Baptist preachers. Let it be remembered that when Cromwell passed away there was little change in this respect. For, six thousand out of the eight thousand clergy who, under Charles IId, occupied the Rectories of England and drew the tithes, were simply Puritans who had "conformed." Hating the Church and Her doctrines and Her discipline while they were under the Commonwealth, how could they love and teach them under the Restoration? The "conforming" Puritan was a man who used the Prayer Book to some extent, but taught the people doctrines antagonistic to its prayers, and practices in violation of its rubrics. Thus, practically, there were, and for a long time continued to be, anomalously enough, two fountains of teaching in the Church. (The Roman part of the Church was similarly afflicted in the eighteenth century.) One of these fountains was the Prayer Book, the other was the pulpit. The Prayer Book, which contains the teaching of the Church, did not hold its own, as a teacher, against the pulpit, which poured forth Puritanism to the people. It is not strange, in the secular confusion of the day, that it was some time before this state of things could be reversed ; that it should be a slow process for the silent Prayer Book to begin to tell at last in the Church against the persistent voice of the pulpit. The pulpit has a way of sending its teachings and its teachers into the Theological Schools, and thus of perpetuating its notions, and keeping them for a while, even on the Episcopal Bench. The secular confusion of the time paralyzed the arm of that discipline which is the mother of order in the Church. Besides, an individual, here and there, may change his belief quickly, but a nation, once indoctrinated, changes its belief slowly. Whatever the Prayer Book may have taught, the English people, once fairly in the current of Puritanism, floated heavily and with steady momentum down that current through the eighteenth century. Let it be remembered, that, forty years after Cromwell, there were Bishops on the English Church thrones who denied Episcopacy, were opposed to the surplice, sustained sectarians, loved even Unitarianism, counseled the abolition of Episcopacy in Scotland, and were opposed to the Thirty-nine Articles. And then consider the state of things in the reigns of the Georges; and it will no longer seem incredible that the members of a National Church can for a while hold doctrines quite different from those held by the Church to which they nominally belong. But at last the Prayer Book began to turn the tide, and to send those it had indoctrinated into the pulpit.

The intent of the Catholic movement of to-day is not to Catholicize the Anglican Church; She has always continued Catholic. But it is to awaken Her members to the Catholic character of their Church.

The Oxford Divines may not have forecast, at the time they issued the "Tracts," the full grandeur of the Revolution they had inaugurated; they may not have anticipated the many nooks and departments of inner spiritual life and of outer human need, into which the new movement would eventually roll and break with upheaving effect. But they comprehended, at any rate, its main purport.

That the Oxford Tracts should rouse violent opposition was of course to be expected. It seemed an easy thing to stamp the new movement down and out of existence. And indeed the heaviest odds were, and have continued to be, against it. But, as that which began to be preached by the Holy Apostles in the year 33 (although the power of the Roman Empire was hurled upon it to crush it), exhibited, nevertheless, a stubborn life and an ever increasing growth, so this, which began to be preached in the year 1833, has exhibited the same phenomena of life and growth. Why is this? Simply because the movement of 1833 is but a resurrection of the movement of A. D. 33. In the sixteenth century, the thinking world rejected that adulterated presentment of Christianity known as Romanism; because it was tyranny. In the nineteenth century the thinking world has rejected that other adulterated presentment of Christianity known as Protestantism; because it is utter anarchy. Is it not possible that that ancient Catholicity, which is neither Roman nor Protestant, and which once conquered the world in less than four centuries, should, now that it has roused from its long obscurity, regain that world again which Romanism and Protestantism have between them lost? We see what Romanism and Protestantism have done in a thousand years. Is it unreasonable to ask that the third presentment of Christianity, which was once victorious, be tried again for a century or two?

When such an exceptional movement as this Cath

olic revival takes place, there comes a time at last when its honest and earnest-minded opponents pause in their opposition, and ask " What does it mean?" Such a time as that is dawning now. Already there are some persons, and their number is yearly increasing, who, even though they do not propose to become Catholics, are ready to listen dispassionately to an answer to the question, " What is the object and meaning of this movement?" You, as Evangelicals, have asked this question through your Rector, and you have at once made one at home among you, who comes, not in the spirit of a propagandist, but to speak to brethren who will kindly listen, even though they may continue to differ with him.

At the outset one asks himself, Is there not some single statement, that will comprise within its scope the object of the Catholic movement? If there be such statement, it is perhaps this, namely: The main purport of the Catholic movement, is the re-preaching of the doctrine of the Incarnation in its integrity ; and then come, logically, the practical application of that doctrine to public and private worship, its interior application to the spiritual life of the soul, and its exterior application to the modes in which misery, poverty and sin are to be treated. Of course this practical appli cation strikes against old modes and habits and prejudices with uprooting effect.

Unswerving fidelity to the true doctrine of the Incarnation accounts for every new energy the movement has put forth; for every unexpected angle at which its intense forces have darted out; for every book of devotion it has printed; for every altar-candle it has lighted; for every community of Sisters or Brothers it has organized; for every Early Father it has translated; for every reversal it has made from Choral Matins and plain Celebration, to plain Matins and Choral Celebration; for the extemporaneous mode of preaching it has adopted in place of preaching from a manuscript; for every theological book and pamphlet it has written; for every censer it has swung; for every mission it has preached to sinners, and every quiet and holy retreat it has held for earnest souls; for every Altar and Church it has restored and glorified; for every confession it has heard; for every guild for work among the poor it has organized; for every Early Communion it has celebrated; and every laboring man's club and reading-room it has opened; for every Three Hours Agony Service it has held; every bannered and vestmented procession it has thrown out on Good Fridays into the slums of cities ; every confraternity for combined prayer it has formed; every point of asceticism it has urged ; every public Meditation it has given; every cassock and chasuble it has worn ; every convent and school, the corner stone of which it has laid ; and for every act of voluntary poverty or self-sacrifice of any kind it has undertaken. Undying fidelity to that truth accounts for the turmoils at St. George's in the East; for Pusey silenced in his pulpit ; for Keble banished to the seclusion of a country village, and going to his grave without ecclesiastical preferment or higher collegiate degree; for Bennett hurried away by friends from the mob; for Purchas cut down in the prime of life and sent to his grave ; for Mahan crossing an ocean to defend himself before the Trustees of the General Theological Seminary in the matter of hearing confessions; for Mackonochie suspended and silenced again and again ; for the laboring men going forth from the "Pooh! pooh!" of the Archbishop of Canterbury out of Lambeth Palace gates, and organizing by thousands in every town of England for the defence of Catholicity ; and last and latest, for Arthur Tooth's utterance to the Bishop of Rochester, "I will not obey your civil court; for I will not render unto Cæsar the things that are God's."

The movement has never been understood by its opponents, and they have struggled against it wildly. They have resisted its logical conclusions instead of grappling with its central premise. The issue is between Rationalism and Supernaturalism.

For three hundred years, the popular Religions of the day had been subtly undermining the true doctrine of the Incarnation, until that doctrine had virtually disappeared from the belief of Churchmen. It followed from this popular teaching, indirectly, indeed, but surely, that there was, after all, "little reason for the Son of God becoming man, other than that He might have a human body in which to satisfy the requirement of the Jewish Law, that without shedding of blood there is no remission."* No sermon was a sermon unless the rays of its thoughts were made to converge at last on the Atonement of Calvary and that alone. We were, indeed, lost without the blessed Atonement; but fatal error came under its holy garments.

First, as a corollary of this preaching of the Atonement only, subjective faith in the Atoning Blood,— *i. e.*, a tearful interior apprehension by the sinner that Christ died for him personally on the Cross, was urged

* The London "Church Review."

universally, perpetually, and to all practical intents exclusively on the acceptance of man. Without this faith he had nothing; with it he had all. This could not, and did not fail to obscure, to greater or less degree, the necessity of good works. Nightly self-examination as to what, precisely, one's acts and thoughts and words had been each day, sank into logical unimportance and finally into neglect. The general impression that one was a sinner, took the place of knowledge of one's particular sins; acknowledgment and confession that one was a sinner, took the place of acknowledgment and confession of one's sins. Absolution of one's sins became logically unnecessary; care over the soul, sick with definite sins, attacked with definite temptations, and the nursing and training of the sin-sick soul ceased with the fall of the lesser Sacrament of Absolution; carelessness of watch over acts and words and thoughts, grew to greater or less extent, until at last we have the wide-spread result in fearful national statistics.

Then again, it was man's spirit alone that could exercise this required interior apprehension and this application of the Atonement to one's self. Hence the spirit came to be all in all in the matter of salvation, and the body nothing, as either an aid or a hin drance, in making one's calling and election sure. It is the old story of an excess of one truth, unmodified and unrestrained by another, resulting in error. A thousand salutary restraints of the body, therefore, disappeared. The eye, the ear, the hand, the tongue were neglected. Fasting fell into desuetude; for the body had little or nothing to do with that "Spiritual" religion which was summed up in merely apprehending Christ as one's Saviour, and so being saved. St. Paul's "I keep my body under and bring it into subjection," "in watchings often, in fastings often," "lest when I have preached to others, I myself should be a castaway," grew to be a dead letter. Christ's "This kind goeth not out but by prayer and fasting," was as though He had never said it.

Furthermore, what was called "spiritual worship" took the place of the worship of the whole man in body and soul. Forms, liturgies and the Visible Church disappeared; for matter had been deconsecrated; churches fell into decay and squalor; and the worship of Almighty God was made cold and gloomy to the heart of child and man, and contemptible in the eyes of the world. Families became prayerless. Time was, when nobody thought of going to bed at night or rising in the morning without saying his prayers. Now, not merely thousands but millions in England, America and Germany, go prayerless to bed, and rise in the morning and enter prayerless upon a new day. With decay of worship came, as a matter of course, decay of godliness, with all its attendant evils; the absence of the poor from God's house, the neglect of the poor, their ignorance and practical heathenism.

Then again, with faith in the Atoning Cross the solitary thing needful, a mere natural memory of the past tragedy on Calvary took the place of the supernatural and perpetually recurring Sacrifice of the Altar, in which is presented, in a Consecration Prayer addressed to Almighty God (and not in a mere instruction to man) a Memorial to God the Father. "Wherefore with these Thy Holy Gifts which we offer unto Thee, we do make here *before Thy Divine Majesty*, the Memorial Thy Son hath commanded us to make." The five lesser Sacraments fell out entirely from Christianity; and the whole character of Sunday assemblages changed. Instead of presenting to the world a solemn, Sacrificial and Sacramental worship offered to Almighty God, they presented the aspect of a congregation seated before a pulpit from which the all-sufficient Justification by faith in the Atonement was sol emnly and impressively urged. As a logical consequence, sermons increased in number, and men began to abolish the only service the Lord had especially commanded; Eucharists sank from daily to weekly, from weekly to monthly, from monthly to quarterly, from quarterly, in some cases to yearly or less seldom, and with the Friends they disappeared entirely. Men love Christ, and will always crowd to Him when He comes; but with the Real Presence of Christ banished from the Altar, and with the disappearance of the Altar itself, Sunday assemblages grew thinner except under the electrical power of the popular preacher, always a rare personage. Daily prayer ceased; and churches were closed six days out of the seven. With the fall of prayers, public and private, and of the Sacrament of the Altar, the Sacrament of Baptism fell also. Time was, when every child was of course baptised. From a holy and tremendous thing, Baptism, though solemnly commanded by God, fell logically in the estimation of the masses into a mere form by no means of great importance. A comparatively non-church-going community became, to a large extent, not only a prayerless community but also one thoughtless of religious subjects and careless of religious truth. And then followed the consequences:

worldliness, the hasting to be rich, extravagance, gambling, defalcations, bribery, divorces, infanticide and fœticide; Roman Catholics left mainly to populate the country with their children, through our great Herodian sin.

Again, if a man was saved when he could at last by an interior process apprehend the Saviour as dying on the Cross for him personally, what more was needed? Saved is saved; full is full. The distinction, therefore, between the precepts for all and the counsels for the few who can bear them, disappeared from the public apprehension. Efforts, therefore, after any higher life by rare souls ceased; and, as a matter of course, Sisterhoods and Brotherhoods, which are built upon that distinction, became an impertinence, and at last an offence. Hence that ethereal phenomenon in the soul, rare sanctity, as distinguished from eminent moral goodness, disappeared. With the disappearance of the skilled religious, as practical agents, as the right and left arms of the Church, and with that training and life of theirs abolished which makes them skilled, a crude and mercenary, a comparatively ineffective, expensive and malapert treatment of misery, poverty, illness and ignorance followed.

II. But time forbids that we should go on and trace all the steps of disaster and decay leading out from a false view of the Incarnation.

Nay, there were other and great reasons for the Son of God becoming man than that He might merely possess a human body in which to be crucified, and then leave a Bible and a pulpit behind Him. And the object of the Catholic movement, from its first phase in 1833 to its last to-day, is to re-preach and to restore, in all its practical applications and consequences, the true doctrine of the Incarnation. Having considered the process of decay, let us now consider some of the steps in the process of reconstruction.

Many excellent people suppose that this great Catholic movement begins and ends in Ritualism. Ritual is not, indeed, utterly unimportant. As the stars and stripes stood, in the late war, as a symbol of the great principles of nationality and union, so that if any one hauled them down he was to be "shot on the spot," so analogously is it with Ritual. But although it is of less importance than other things in the movement, permit me first to say a word or two on Ritual, since it is that part of the movement which is most conspicuous to the world, and has led the world to misunderstand and belittle the great movement itself.

It is to be remembered that the true doctrine of the Incarnation involves many things; more than can now be enumerated. But one of those things is this, namely: the Incarnation,—the Son of God descending and taking to Himself man's nature, with human body and soul subsisting,—means, not only the reconsecration of the soul, but also the reconsecration both of the body and of all matter to the service and glory of God. That on Mount Tabor the Flesh of the Lord was transfigured we readily remember; but it is an amazing thought that the very earthly garments He wore were also transfigured. As, then, one result of the Incarnation was the reconsecration both of the body and of all matter to the service and glory of God, it was logically inevitable, "that this great Catholic movement should make a place in itself somewhere for external Ritual." And Ritual has been defended by Catholics when it has been attacked, it has been more firmly insisted on when ridiculed, because they cannot permit the capture of any outwork in the unbroken circle of those defences which guard the vital central doctrine of the Incarnation. The old yellow and white-wash, which Puritanism applied to church walls, is therefore scraped off; churches are restored; Altars are set up and glorified with lights and embroidery and gold, with spotless linen, the flower, the garnet and the emerald ; vestments are worn ; congregations *kneel;* and, in general, the public worship of God is made more glorious and grand by song and procession and adoration ; for in the Incarnation the body of man is reconsecrated as a creature of God to the glory of its Maker. "Thou shalt worship the Lord thy God ;" "Vouchsafe to direct, sanctify and govern" (not only our hearts, but) "our bodies" (also) "in the ways of Thy Laws."

But there is also involved in the re-preaching of the Incarnation what is of more importance: *i. e.* the reappearance and the nurture of that Supernatural and Sacramental phenomenon, the Inner Spiritual Life of the Soul. When this Spiritual life is well developed, we have something higher than mere goodness, and different in quality. We have Sainthood. Sainthood does not pause at eminent morality, but taking it for its starting point goes on to something more ethereal.

What is this Spiritual life? It is the union within each man of the Divine Life with the human. That union began in the God-Man, and is imparted to each of us through Baptism. That is to say, Almighty God, having in the Incarnation imparted the Divine

Nature to the Human, so that the two should be one in the Person of Christ, extends the process by which the Divine Nature is incarnated, by planting a germ of that Christ-nature in each other human soul at Baptism; so that Christ becomes "one flesh" not only in an abstract sense with mankind, but concretely with each human being, to whom at first He gave His nature in germ, and then afterwards feeds it with His Body and Blood. Thus His Body Natural grows out and becomes His Body Mystical, the Church. This germ, entering into the Soul and becoming one with it, becomes its divine and Supernatural life. Without it the soul possesses only its natural and moral life, and is therefore dead supernaturally.

Now this spiritual life is, I say, to be imparted after birth to the soul. It is to be superadded to the moral life which we get from Adam. It is given by God in Baptism. Hence there is involved in the re-preaching of the Incarnation a revival also of the Sacrament of Baptism as a tremendous supernatural reality, as an agent through which God works on earth.

This sacramental, supernatural life is afterwards to be strengthened, nurtured, developed; otherwise it will remain in its mere germ state, to all practical intents useless. Hence there is involved in the re-preaching of the Incarnation the revival of the other Sacraments, the five lesser as well as the two greater. For, first, this spiritual life must be strengthened; hence more care by Catholics in the matter of Confirmation. It must also be fed with appropriate Spiritual food; hence the Catholic movement calls back the Blessed Sacrament of the Altar from yearly celebrations to monthly, to weekly, to daily.

But you may ask, How happens it that the Sacrament of Absolution is revived, and the rubric in the English Prayer Book concerning confession is obeyed once more, instead of remaining a dead letter? The answer is as follows: It is the distinguishing feature and consummate blessing of the Incarnation, with its necessary Sacramental System, that it brings God into actual contact with man. This contact occurred first in the God-Man; and is extended to us through the Sacraments. It is in the Sacraments that we touch God. It is in Baptism that the Divine germ passes into incorporation with the Soul. It is in Communion that real contact between Christ and the Soul takes place, so that each shall not only touch, but dwell in the other. It is in Confirmation that the Holy Ghost is in contact with the Soul. So, too, there is the contact between God and the Soul in the Sacrament of

Absolution. Hence confession in that Sacrament is perceived to be the true, direct and immediate confession to God, which Christianity and Christianity only vouchsafes; while confession in the closet, instead of being the direct, is after all that indirect and distant mode of confession to God, which the heathen and the infidel could always have used, and which the non-christian can use to-day; it is not distinctively Christian. It is the way of natural religion. But nay, think we, Christianity vouchsafes some higher and better and more immediate and holier privilege than Natural Religion or heathenism could boast. It is a layman's question; no one has a right to compel any one to confess; and if a man wishes to confess, no one has a right to deprive him of his right. And the laymen in England and America, in increasing thousands, are rising and demanding their right to confess (as they feel) directly to God in His Sacrament of Absolution, in which He vouchsafes contact with man; and to receive absolution directly from God in that Sacrament through the hands of their Priests. We go to Penance, not in order to confess our sins to a man; but rather do we go to confess our sins in a Holy Sacrament to God.

Again, this Sacramental life must be trained

Merely preaching to it may instruct, and please, but it does not train, assist, guide and discipline it in the use of its faculties. The little child, the apprentice, needs to be trained and helped, not simply to be talked to. The spiritual life is awkward at first. How to resist different kinds of temptations, how to accquire the use of its newly-given and germinal faculties, how to overcome different sins and shades and combinations of sins, is not known to it by instinct. The Christian life has been called by great Saints a difficult trade to learn; with labor, in much awkwardness at first, and with persistent care and patience. Now the detection of Spiritual diseases and their combinations, and the adjustment to each disease of its various remedies and combination of remedies, are not known to the soul by instinct; a thousand mistakes have been made in the past eighteen centuries in these respects, and, having been discovered to be mistakes, need not be made again. It is barbarism for each generation, and for each man, ignoring the past, to begin all over again where the previous generation began, in the treatment of his spiritual case. It were like abolishing the medical profession and medical libraries, and each man in his ignorance and unskillfulness treating himself when sick physically. Hence there is further involved in the re-preaching of the Incarnation, that revival of the whole science of Ascetic and Moral Theology which the Catholic movement is effecting; a department of theology which treats of the cure of sin and spiritual disease.

Hence, too, there follows a restoration of the clergy from their position as mere preachers and social visitors, to their Apostolic and Catholic position as Priests, as trainers and physicians of the Spiritual life. There follows also a revival of the sharp distinction between clergy and laity, and of the tender relationship of clerical Fatherhood and lay Sonship, with that perfect confidence between confessor and penitent which their mutual silence alone could give; a silence as deep as that of the interstellar spaces. The Catholic Church is one continuous, visible, organic Body, the invisible Soul of Which is the God-Man, Christ. If Christ is not in and one with the Catholic Church, as a soul is in and one with its body, then the Church is a dead body. But if Christ is literally on earth in His Body Mystical, the Church, to suppose that He cannot speak the word of pardon to the kneeling, repentant, confessing sinner, is to suppose that Christ is, as to one of the organs of His Body Mystical and Visible, stricken with paralysis.

Involved in all the above is necessarily the revival also of daily self-examination, of counsel and direction, of the strengthening aid of specific penances, each appropriate to its end in the soul. Thus the Catholic movement centres all its efforts and subordinates all its means, external and internal, upon the inner divine life of the soul, to rectify and to build it up in true sanctity, in humility, meekness, charity, patience and purity. All this, too, accounts for the missions which Catholics preach to the careless and the sinner; and for the retreats they hold for clergy, for merchants, for women, for clerks, for the laboring man; that the earnest soul may take account of itself and deepen its spiritual life.

Again, if sins are the sickness and death of the spiritual life, they come through temptation; and temptations reach the soul through the body. The senses are open doors through which they enter. Hence the re-preaching of the Incarnation involves a restoration again of the restraint of the body, which is another phenomenon of the movement. The eye, the ear, the tongue, the touch, the taste, must be guarded, restrained and trained; the feet, that they walk not to sin; the hands, that they search not for sin. This involves also the revival of fasting, and indeed of all other points of asceticism which Catholicity urges. Crucify thyself, crucify thyself; "If thou wouldst indeed see clearly," she cries, "pluck out thine eyes and become blind. If thou wouldst hear well, be deaf. If thou wouldst speak well, be dumb. If thou wouldst walk well, cut off thy feet. If thou wouldst love well, hate thyself. If thou wouldst work well, cut off thy hands. If thou wouldst live well, make thyself die. If thou wouldst gain, learn to lose. If thou wouldst be rich, become poor. If thou wouldst live in pleasure, afflict thyself. If thou wouldst be secure, have perpetual fear. If thou wouldst be honored, despise thyself and honor those who despise thee. If thou wouldst be at rest, work."

Again, if it follows from and is involved in the doctrine of the Incarnation that the Holy Sacraments are the medicine and the strengthening food of the Spiritual life, it equally follows that prayer is the very breath of its existence. Catholicity, therefore, unlooses the tongue of prayer once more. The Confraternity of the Blessed Sacrament and other Confraternities are formed for combined prayer; churches are re-opened on week-days for Daily Morning and Evening Prayer and for private prayer and meditation. This accounts, too, for the fact that Catholicity has flooded our church bookstores with hundreds of new books of sweetest and most varied devotions; treasuries, litanies, chaplets, crowns, and rosaries of prayer follow each other in quick profusion. This, too, accounts for the further phenomenon of the setting up again of the lost arts of mental prayer, of Meditation, and of Contemplation, of Spiritual Communion, of recollection, and of the application of the senses to spiritual objects. For while by nature the senses, and the soul's four faculties of memory, understanding, affections, and will, are ever busying themselves on earthly things and themes, and so taking an earthly hue and fabric, Catholicity teaches not only the four faculties but even the senses also to apply themselves to spiritual objects; to Christ, His words, works, birth, death, and all His other mysteries; in order that the soul, the senses, the whole man, indeed, may become, so to speak, steeped and saturated with the things of spirit and of Heaven, and not be left taking the hue and fabric of the things only of earth and of time. Who ever, in the Georgian Era, heard of such things as Scientific Meditation, Spiritual Communion and the application of the senses to spirit? Verily the last half of the nineteenth century is witnessing a religious revolution, destined to add once more to the

Kalendar of the Saints. With the restoration of fasting and prayer follows of course the observance of Fridays, Lent, the Ember days, and indeed of the whole Kalendar. Again are the English and other Saints thought of, and their lives lifted out of forgetfulness. No longer can it be said, our Mother, the Church, sorrowfully buries Her illustrious children, and we, their brothers, make haste to cast away all tender mementoes of them, and take pride in obliterating even their names and memories.

Again, if the Holy Sacraments are the medicine and food of the spiritual life and prayer the very breath of its existence, it equally follows that practical works, in all the fourteen spiritual and corporal deeds of mercy, are its exercise, absolutely necessary to its vigor and health. I know that this suggests at once those other phenomena of the movement, not only the revival of Sisterhoods and Brotherhoods, but also the new-born energy with which the movement has planted its Churches in the purlieus of cities; organized workingmen's guilds, clubs and reading rooms, convalescent homes, *creches*, indeed the hundred and one new appliances of practical good which have sprung up under the magic wand of—"mere Ritualism and nonsense."

But a word, at least, in passing, on the occult current that has led out from the Incarnation into all this practical energy among the poor and suffering and ignorant. The moment the true doctrine of the Incarnation, with its spiritual life and its Sacraments, rises before the mind, that moment there springs up again, by necessity, from its fallen estate the distinction between precepts and counsels, which are the rules of the spiritual life, and which divide it into its two departments, the Religious life, namely, of the Sister and the Brother, and the secular life of the ordinary Christian who lives in the world. And then, with communities of Religious restored to the Church, something else of the greatest value follows and is restored also. For, by an inevitable process, too long to describe now, a spiritual stamina and sustained power are accumulated in the Sisters and Brothers, and a corresponding new-born practical skill in the exercise of the works of mercy is acquired by them; a stamina and skill which do not confine themselves to the Sisterhoods and Brotherhoods, but which, partly through the instruction and example of the Regulars and partly by a use of the same new spiritual causes that have given them this skill and stamina, flow down to some extent and spread through the secular part of the Church also. So that both Regulars and Seculars (or the Trained and the Untrained), rousing with a new energy and hope, go forth hand in hand to the work among the poor, the ignorant and the afflicted, with that aptitude, faculty, sustained power, and self-sacrificing spirit, with that love of God and of man, and with that marvellous effectiveness, which have marked the movement more and more as time advances, and to which the Church had been a stranger for over two centuries. Behold earnest Bishops beginning to be desirous of having Sisters work in their dioceses. Verily there is a change since that time when one of the earliest of our Sisters entered St. Alban's Church, Holborn, covered from bonnet to the skirts of her dress with the spittle of the mob.

Much more might be said. The Sacrificial aspect of the Blessed Eucharist; the charity of prayers for the dead which is due from the living, and the Christian fine arts have not been forgotten; but this discourse already taxes the patience by its length. Nor is the adoration paid by Catholics to Our Blessed Lord present in His Holy Sacrament forgotten. I may visit a person's library for the purpose of procuring a book; but, though I did not go merely for wishing him the compliments of the day, I should nevertheless be deemed guilty of a great discourtesy should I not salute him in the customary manner on entering. And so the Catholic feels, that even though he approaches the Lord for the purpose of receiving the inestimable bounty of His Body and Blood, to do so without offering incidentally that solemn, adoring salutation which is due from the creature to his God, would be, to say the least, not the highest instinct of tenderness, of recollection, and of humility. John Keble has said that it seems to him as impossible for Faith, as it beholds Christ in the Blessed Eucharist, to keep from adoring Him, as it is for a mother to help loving her child when she contemplates it in its cradle.

But enough has been hinted and suggested, I trust, to show you, that, of all the phenomena of this great revival, not one is fortuitous, not one is erratic, but all grow logically and have come irresistibly out of the re-preaching of the Early Church doctrine of the Incarnation; not even excepting the translation into English of the works of the Early Fathers, that every man may read and see for himself that the Catholic revival is nothing other than the re-birth and re-presentation in its integrity of Early Church and Apos tolic Catholic Christianity, which has been in some vital respects fearfully contorted by Rome, and in others destroyed by Protestantism.

THE END.

www.ingramcontent.com/pod-product-compliance
Lightning Source LLC
Chambersburg PA
CBHW021955220426
43663CB00007B/821